Nicotine Addiction
Among Adolescents

Nicotine Addiction Among Adolescents has been co-published simultaneously as *Journal of Child & Adolescent Substance Abuse,* Volume 9, Number 4 2000.

The *Journal of Child & Adolescent Substance Abuse* Monographic "Separates"

Below is a list of "separates," which in serials librarianship means a special issue simultaneously published as a special journal issue or double-issue *and* as a "separate" hardbound monograph. (This is a format which we also call a "DocuSerial.")

"Separates" are published because specialized libraries or professionals may wish to purchase a specific thematic issue by itself in a format which can be separately cataloged and shelved, as opposed to purchasing the journal on an on-going basis. Faculty members may also more easily consider a "separate" for classroom adoption.

"Separates" are carefully classified separately with the major book jobbers so that the journal tie-in can be noted on new book order slips to avoid duplicate purchasing.

You may wish to visit Haworth's website at . . .

http://www.haworthpressinc.com

. . . to search our online catalog for complete tables of contents of these separates and related publications.

You may also call 1-800-HAWORTH (outside US/Canada: 607-722-5857), or Fax: 1-800-895-0582 (outside US/Canada: 607-771-0012), or e-mail at:

getinfo@haworthpressinc.com

Nicotine Addiction Among Adolescents, edited by Eric F. Wagner, PhD (Vol. 9, No. 4, 2000). *Containing research and current theories, Nicotine Addiction Among Adolescents offers researchers and medical professionals insight into emerging practices and methods of treating nicotine addiction in adolescents and thus help them stop smoking.*

The Etiology and Prevention of Drug Abuse Among Minority Youth, edited by Gilbert J. Botvin, PhD, and Steven Schinke, PhD (Vol. 6, No. 1 1997). *"Provides information on the causes of drug use among minority adolescents, the strengths and limitations of different intervention approaches, and ways to work appropriately with at-risk minority teens." (American Public Welfare Association)*

Nicotine Addiction Among Adolescents

Eric F. Wagner, PhD
Editor

Nicotine Addiction Among Adolescents has been co-published simultaneously as *Journal of Child & Adolescent Substance Abuse,* Volume 9, Number 4 2000.

The Haworth Press, Inc.
New York • London • Oxford

Nicotine Addiction Among Adolescents has been co-published simultaneously as *Journal of Child & Adolescent Substance Abuse,* Volume 9, Number 4 2000.

The Haworth Press, Inc., 10 Alice Street, Binghamton, NY 13904-1580 USA

Cover design by Thomas J. Mayshock Jr.

Library of Congress Cataloging-in-Publication Data

Nicotine addiction among adolescents/Eric F. Wagner, editor.
    p. cm.
   Includes bibliographical references and index.
   ISBN 0-7890-1170-0 (alk. paper)–ISBN 0-7890-1171-9 (alk. paper)
    1. Teenagers–Tobacco use. 2. Tobacco habit–Prevention. I. Wagner, Eric F.

HV5745.N53 2000
362.29'6'0853–dc21

00-038851

Indexing, Abstracting & Website/Internet Coverage

This section provides you with a *chronological list* of major indexing & abstracting services. That is to say, each service began covering this periodical during the year noted in the right column. Most Websites which are listed below have indicated that they will either post, disseminate, compile, archive, cite or alert their own Website users with research-based content from this work. (This list is as current as the copyright date of this publication.)

Abstracting, Website/Indexing Coverage .... Year When Coverage Began

- *ERIC CLEARINGHOUSE ON COUNSELING AND STUDENT SERVICES (ERIC/CASS)* 1993

- *ACADEMIC ABSTRACTS/CD-ROM* 1994

- *ALCONLINE DATABASE* 1994

- *BIOLOGY DIGEST* 1994

- *BROWN UNIVERSITY DIGEST OF ADDICTION THEORY AND APPLICATION, THE (DATA Newsletter)* 1994

- *CAMBRIDGE SCIENTIFIC ABSTRACTS* 1994

- *CHILD DEVELOPMENT ABSTRACTS & BIBLIOGRAPHY* ... 1994

- *CINAHL (Cumulative Index to Nursing & Allied Health Literature), in print, also on CD-ROM from CD PLUS, EBSCO, and SilverPlatter, and online from CDP Online (formerly BRS), Data-Star, and PaperChase. (Support materials include Subject Heading List, Database Search Guide, and instructional video.)* 1994

- *CRIMINAL JUSTICE ABSTRACTS* 1994

(continued)

(continued)

Special Bibliographic Notes related to special journal issues (separates) and indexing/abstracting:

- indexing/abstracting services in this list will also cover material in any "separate" that is co-published simultaneously with Haworth's special thematic journal issue or DocuSerial. Indexing/abstracting usually covers material at the article/chapter level.
- monographic co-editions are intended for either non-subscribers or libraries which intend to purchase a second copy for their circulating collections.
- monographic co-editions are reported to all jobbers/wholesalers/approval plans. The source journal is listed as the "series" to assist the prevention of duplicate purchasing in the same manner utilized for books-in-series.
- to facilitate user/access services all indexing/abstracting services are encouraged to utilize the co-indexing entry note indicated at the bottom of the first page of each article/chapter/contribution.
- this is intended to assist a library user of any reference tool (whether print, electronic, online, or CD-ROM) to locate the monographic version if the library has purchased this version but not a subscription to the source journal.
- individual articles/chapters in any Haworth publication are also available through the Haworth Document Delivery Service (HDDS).

Nicotine Addiction Among Adolescents

CONTENTS

ABOUT THE EDITOR

Eric F. Wagner, PhD, is Associate Professor in the College of Urban and Public Affairs at Florida International University and a licensed psychologist in the State of Florida. Dr. Wagner received his doctoral degree in Clinical Psychology from the University of Pittsburgh, and he completed post-doctoral fellowship at the Brown University Center for Alcohol and Addiction Studies. His interests are in the areas of adolescent substance abuse and the empirical evaluation of psychotherapeutic interventions. He has published numerous scholarly articles and chapters in these areas, and he has received grants from the National Institutes of Health to examine risk factors for and the treatment of adolescent substance use problems.

Introduction

Eric F. Wagner

SUMMARY. Adolescent smoking has increasingly become a topic of interest and research in the addiction field. Epidemiological studies have demonstrated that most adolescents try smoking, over one-third become daily smokers, and nearly one quarter become addicted to cigarettes. While significant recent gains have been made in understanding and treating nicotine addiction among adults, similar gains have not been made in understanding and treating nicotine addiction among adolescents. Much work remains to be done concerning the developmental appropriateness and usefulness of conceptualizations, methods, and strategies initially developed for adult smoking. *[Article copies available for a fee from The Haworth Document Delivery Service: 1-800-342-9678. E-mail address: <getinfo@haworthpressinc.com> Website: <http://www.haworthpressinc.com>]*

KEYWORDS. Smoking, adolescence, nicotine addiction

The past decade has seen increasing interest in preventing and treating cigarette smoking among teenagers. Recent epidemiological data have indi-

Eric F. Wagner, PhD, is affiliated with the College of Urban and Public Affairs, Florida International University.

Address correspondence to Eric F. Wagner, PhD, College of Urban and Public Affairs, Florida International University, North Campus, AC-1, Suite 200, North Miami, FL 33181-3600 (E-mail: wagnere@fiu.edu).

Preparation of this article was supported in part by National Institute on Alcohol Abuse and Alcoholism Grant AA10246.

[Haworth co-indexing entry note]: "Introduction." Wagner, Eric, F. Co-published simultaneously in *Journal of Child & Adolescent Substance Abuse* (The Haworth Press, Inc.) Vol. 9, No. 4, 2000, pp. 1-4; and: *Nicotine Addiction Among Adolescents* (ed: Eric F. Wagner) The Haworth Press, Inc., 2000, pp. 1-4. Single or multiple copies of this article are available for a fee from The Haworth Document Delivery Service [1-800-342-9678, 9:00 a.m. - 5:00 p.m. (EST). E-mail address: getinfo@haworthpressinc.com].

cated that adolescent smoking is prevalent and has been on the rise since the middle 1980s. Estimates of the number of adolescents who will try smoking a cigarette by the time they complete high school range from 65.3% to 70.2% (CDC, 1998a; University of Michigan, 1998). The Centers for Disease Control report that more than one third of students who ever try cigarette smoking will become daily smokers (CDC, 1998a), and Anthony, Warner, and Kessler (1994) report that almost one quarter of students who try smoking ultimately will meet diagnostic criteria for nicotine dependence.

Currently, it is estimated that over one-third of American students smoke by the time they leave high school (University of Michigan, 1999). During the span from 1988-1996, initiation of first use increased by 30% and of first daily use by 50% among persons aged 12-17 years (CDC, 1998b). Moreover, adolescence is the peak developmental period for the initiation of tobacco use, with approximately 80% of first time use occurring among individuals younger than 18 years (US DHHS, 1994). It has been estimated that an adolescent who starts smoking now can expect to continue smoking for at least 16 years if female and 20 years if male (Pierce & Gilpin, 1996).

Smoking among adolescents is a public health priority given the well-documented negative consequences of the behavior. Cigarette smoking is a leading cause of morbidity and mortality in the United States and is the single largest preventable cause of premature death in the United States (USDHHS, 1985, 1989). Approximately one in five deaths in the United States can be attributed to tobacco use (McGinnis & Foege, 1993). Moreover, research has demonstrated that physical damage from smoking begins in adolescence, and occurs even among teens with low levels of smoking (Dwyer, Rieger-Ndakorerwa, Seamer, Fuchs, & Lippert, 1988; US DHHS, 1994).

Despite the prevalence of adolescent smoking and the negative consequences associated with this behavior, the theoretical and empirical literature concerning smoking among teenagers remains skimpy. While we have seen a dramatic increase in empirical research on and effective treatments for nicotine dependence among adults, relatively little has been done with adolescents. Investigators who have worked in the area of smoking among adults are beginning to turn their attention to adolescence, the part of the lifespan where smoking is most likely to start and nicotine addiction is most likely to begin. However, many of the conceptualizations, methods, and strategies used with adult smoking may not adequately address adolescent smoking. Also, some investigators who have worked in the area of adolescent risk behavior are beginning to devote more time to cigarette smoking, but many lack background and expertise in the area of nicotine addiction.

The intent of this work is to provide researchers and clinicians with an overview of current developments and future directions in the area of adolescent smoking and nicotine dependence. In the opening paper, Henningfield,

Michaelides, and Sussman present a comprehensive summary of the current state of affairs in smoking and nicotine dependence research and treatment with adolescents. They identify a host of currently unanswered questions about teenage smoking, each of which will need to be addressed for research and treatment to progress.

The second and third papers consider the appropriateness of the application of concepts and strategies developed with adult smokers to adolescent smokers. Kassel discusses the utility of the concept of nicotine addiction when applied to adolescents, and reviews the theoretical and empirical bases from which inferences regarding addictive smoking in adolescence can be drawn. Patten begins with recent developments in nicotine replacement therapies for adults, and then considers practical and ethical issues associated with applying these treatments to adolescents.

In the fourth paper, Myers, Brown, and Kelly present findings from a study of a psychosocial smoking cessation therapy developed expressly for adolescents. They have piloted this program with substance abusing adolescents, who are the heaviest smoking group of adolescents. In the final paper, Wagner and Atkins focus on smoking among adolescent females. They describe risk factors that may be specific to teenage girls and offer suggestions as to how prevention and intervention programs could be made more effective for females.

In conclusion, I hope that the five papers provoke thought and discussion among practitioners and researchers working in the area of adolescent smoking. For the field to advance, I believe interchange between experts in smoking and experts in adolescent development will be necessary. While there has been a long tradition of developmental sensitivity in approaches to preventing smoking among teenagers, developmentally sensitive approaches to conceptualizing and treating nicotine addiction among adolescents are only just now beginning to appear. To move forward in our understanding and treatment of adolescent smoking, the concepts and approaches of smoking researchers and of adolescent development researchers will need to be merged and integrated. The five papers presented in this work represent early attempts toward such integration, and hopefully will serve as guides and models to future developments in the area.

REFERENCES

Anthony, J.C., Warner, L.A., & Kessler, R.C. (1994). Comparative epidemiology of dependence on tobacco, alcohol, controlled substances and inhalants: Basic findings from the National Comorbidity Study. *Experimental and Clinical Psychopharmacology, 2,* 244-268.

Centers for Disease Control (1998a). Selected cigarette smoking initiation and quitting behaviors among high school students–United States, 1997. *Morbidity and Mortality Weekly Report, 47,* 386-389.

Centers for Disease Control (1998b). Incidence of initiation of cigarette smoking–United States, 1965-1996. *Morbidity and Mortality Weekly Report, 47,* 837-840.

Dwyer, J.H., Rieger-Ndakorerwa, G.E., Seamer, N.K., Fuchs, R., & Lippert, P. (1988). Low-level cigarette smoking and longitudinal change in serum cholesterol among adolescents. *Journal of the American Medical Association, 259,* 2857-2862.

McGinnis, J.M., & Foege, W.H. (1993). Actual causes of death in the United States. *The Journal of the American Medical Assiocation, 270,* 2207-2212.

Pierce, J., & Gilpin, E. (1996). How long will today's new adolescent smoker be addicted to cigarettes? *American Journal of Public Health, 86,* 253-256.

University of Michigan (1998). *Smoking among American teens declines some.* News and Information Services Press Release, December 18, 1998.

U.S. Department of Health and Human Services (1985). *The health consequences of smoking: Cancer and chronic lung disease in the workplace: A report of the Surgeon General.* Rockville, MD: Office on Smoking and Health, U.S. Department of Health and Human Services, Public Health Service.

U.S. Department of Health and Human Services (1989). *Reducing the negative health consequences of smoking: 25 years of progress: A report of the Surgeon General.* Washington, DC: U.S. Department of Health and Human Services, Public Health Service.

U.S. Department of Health and Human Services (1994). *Preventing tobacco use among young people: A report of the Surgeon General.* Atlanta, GA: U.S. Department of Health and Human Services, Public Health Service, Centers for Disease Control.

Developing Treatment
for Tobacco Addicted Youth–
Issues and Challenges

Jack E. Henningfield
Tula Michaelides
Steve Sussman

SUMMARY. It is now clear that adolescence is not only the primary time during which cigarette smoking is initiated; it is also the time during which the transition from experimentation to some level of dependence occurs. As discussed in this review, by age 18 approximately two-thirds of cigarette smokers regret having started smoking, one-half have already made a quit attempt, and nearly 40% have some interest in obtaining treatment for their dependence. Unfortunately, treatment in young people has not kept pace with the emerging need for

Jack E. Henningfield, PhD, is affiliated with Johns Hopkins University School of Medicine, Baltimore, MD and Pinney Associates, Inc., Bethesda, MD. Tula Michaelides, BA, is affiliated with Johns Hopkins University School of Hygiene and Public Health, Baltimore, MD. Steve Sussman, PhD, is affiliated with University of Southern California, Department of Preventive Medicine, and Institute for Health Promotion and Disease Prevention Research.

Address correspondence to Jack E. Henningfield, Vice President, Research and Health Policy, Pinney Associates, Inc., 4800 Montgomery Lane, Suite 1000, Bethesda, MD 20814 (E-mail: jhenning@pinneyassociates.com).

This research was supported in part by grants from the American Cancer Society and the USC Norris Comprehensive Cancer Center and the California Tobacco-Related Disease Research Program (6RT-0182). Dr. Henningfield's and Ms. Michaelides' efforts were supported by funds provided by SmithKline Beecham Consumer Health Care. The authors also express their appreciation to Ms. Lakshmi Gopolan for her assistance in the preparation of this manuscript.

[Haworth co-indexing entry note]: "Developing Treatment for Tobacco Addicted Youth–Issues and Challenges." Henningfield, Jack, E., Tula Michaelides, and Steve Sussman. Co-published simultaneously in *Journal of Child & Adolescent Substance Abuse* (The Haworth Press, Inc.) Vol. 9, No. 4, 2000, pp. 5-26; and: *Nicotine Addiction Among Adolescents* (ed: Eric F. Wagner) The Haworth Press, Inc., 2000, pp. 5-26. Single or multiple copies of this article are available for a fee from The Haworth Document Delivery Service [1-800-342-9678, 9:00 a.m. - 5:00 p.m. (EST). E-mail address: getinfo@haworthpressinc.com].

treatment and many fundamental issues require study; in fact it is not clear the degree to which adult-validated treatments, such as nicotine replacement therapies, will be of comparable levels of benefit and risk in young people. The issues that require research include (1) a thorough consideration of adolescent nicotine dependence and potential pharmacologic adjuncts, (2) a consideration of social, health, risk perception, and intrapersonal factors that may facilitate or inhibit cessation attempts of maintenance among youth, and (3) advanced youth cessation trials research designs and measurement. We conclude that although the research challenges are many and diverse, all are surmountable by concerted efforts, and the opportunity to reduce the current projections of premature tobacco-caused mortality in one-third to one-half of cigarette smoking youth strongly argue for such efforts. *[Article copies available for a fee from The Haworth Document Delivery Service: 1-800-342-9678. E-mail address: <getinfo@haworthpressinc.com> Website: <http://www.haworthpressinc.com>]*

KEYWORDS. Smoking, adolescence, treatment, nicotine dependence

Tobacco use in young people is our nation's major avoidable cause of death, disease and disability. Tobacco's mortality toll among adults exceeds all other forms of drug and alcohol abuse, homicides, traffic accidents, and HIV-related disease combined. Surprisingly, although most smokers begin regular use in adolescence, there has been little effort to develop and provide adolescents with smoking cessation interventions. The perception of the need for smoking cessation interventions for youth is now changing rapidly. This is due, in part, to the growing recognition that many young tobacco users make the transition from experimental use to dependence prior to adulthood. As former Commissioner of the Food and Drug Administration (FDA), Dr. David A. Kessler concluded: "Nicotine addiction begins when most tobacco users are teenagers, so let's call this what it really is: a pediatric disease" (Kessler, 1995a; Kessler et al., 1996). The corollary of this conclusion is that treatment should be available for all those afflicted, and not just adults.

This shift in how tobacco dependence is clinically framed is not novel; Slade and others earlier had come to similar conclusions as Kessler (Slade, 1993; Lynch & Bonnie, 1994; USDHHS, 1994). But Kessler successfully used this conceptualization to support a youth-framed approach to FDA regulation of nicotine as a drug and cigarettes and smokeless tobacco as drug delivery devices (Kessler et al., 1997). These conclusions highlight the needs for treatment development and dissemination to adolescent nicotine-dependent persons.

Stimulated in part by FDA actions, the National Cancer Institute launched a program to stimulate and fund research concerning "the prevention and cessation of tobacco use by children and youth in the U.S." in 1997, and again in 1998. Additionally, the Centers for Disease Control and Prevention's Office on Smoking and Health initiated its own program to assess and address the treatment needs of nicotine dependent youth with its Youth Tobacco Cessation Meeting in 1997, and the Robert Wood Johnson Foundation, (Princeton, New Jersey) made an eight-year commitment to fund a research network on the etiology of nicotine dependence in youth. Thus, it would be reasonable to expect increasing research on the understanding and treatment of pediatric nicotine dependence. Nonetheless, developing and evaluating treatment strategies for tobacco-addicted youth pose many issues and challenges to researchers and our nation's treatment infrastructure alike. The purpose of the present paper is to discuss these issues.

TRENDS IN PREVALENCE OF YOUTH TOBACCO USE: IMPLICATIONS FOR TREATMENT

Youth use of tobacco declined in the 1970s, stabilized in the 1980s, and has steadily increased since 1992 (Centers for Disease Control and Prevention (CDC), 1998). In contrast, adult smoking declined in the 1980s and leveled off in the mid-1990s. The first signs of a leveling off in tobacco-attributed deaths were detected in 1991, but this may not continue if current tobacco-use trends among youth are not reversed (USDHHS, 1993). This is tragic because approximately one-half of unremitting smokers prematurely die of smoking-caused disease (Peto, Lopez, Boreham, Thun & Heath Jr., 1994). Correspondingly, at least one-third of youth who begin smoking will prematurely die of smoking-caused disease (FDA, 1995).

Recent trends in adolescent tobacco use do not bode well. Smoking among high school seniors was at an all-time high of 36.9% in 1997; and since 1991, past-month smoking has increased by 35% among eighth graders and 43% among tenth graders. Nearly a third of high school seniors (31.6%) who smoke a pack or more of cigarettes per day are still smoking five years later. This percentage is 41.6% for those who smoke about half a pack a day, and 84.8% for nondaily smokers (Pierce & Giplin, 1996; US DHHS, 1994).

Another change in youth tobacco use involves smokeless forms of tobacco. In the 1970s, most smokeless tobacco users were men 50 years-old or older (US DHHS, 1994). Less than 1% of all youth (less than 2% of male youth) used smokeless tobacco products, and there was not a strong base of initiation among adults who had not previously used tobacco products (Connolly et al., 1986; Sussman et al., 1995). By the late 1980s, the demographics of smokeless tobacco use had been reversed. There was a 1,500% increase in prevalence of smokeless tobacco use among 18-19 year olds (US DHHS, 1994). The highest prevalence of use was in boys and younger men; the lowest prevalence of use was in men over 50 and females. Moreover, this explosive increase in smokeless tobacco use did not come at the expense of cigarette smoking. Rather, smokeless tobacco use developed in addition to cigarette smoking, and even seemed to provide an additional gateway to smoking, as discussed in the 1988 and 1994 Surgeon General's Reports (US DHHS, 1988; 1994; Henningfield, Clayton & Pollin, 1990).

Cigar smoking is the most recently documented form of increasing tobacco use among youth. Data from the 1997 Youth Risk Behavior Survey showed that "past 30 day cigar smoking prevalence among males was 31%, and nearly 11% of females had smoked a cigar in the past month" (Gerlach et al., 1998). Between 1986-1992, older males were more likely than younger males to have ever smoked cigars, but there was an increase in prevalence of cigar smoking among younger, 18-24 year old males between 1992-1993 and 1995-1996. Overall, cigar smoking increased nearly 50% from 1993 to 1997 (Gerlach et al., 1998). Moreover, cigar smoking youth, as are smokeless tobacco using youth, are much more likely to smoke cigarettes, drink alcohol, and smoke marijuana than are non-cigar and non-smokeless tobacco users (Gerlach et al., 1998).

Yet another troubling trend relates to tobacco use by minority youth. In the 1970s and 1980s, the 1998 Surgeon General's Report on Tobacco Use Among U.S. Racial/Ethnic Minority Groups reported that smoking rates declined substantially among African American youths regardless of gender, self-reported school performance, parental education, and personal income (US DHHS, 1998). However, these rates have increased markedly since 1992. Specifically, smoking rates have grown by a startling rate of 80% among African American youth from 1991 to 1997. If these trends continue, about 1.6 million African Americans now under the age of 18 will become regular smokers, and about 500,000 of them will die of a smoking-related disease. During the same period of time, smoking among Hispanic high school students increased by 34%. Analogous changes in smoking-related mortality can be predicted. Taken together, these trends indicate rapidly increasing rates of tobacco use among youth.

NEED FOR YOUTH TOBACCO USE CESSATION PROGRAMMING

The need for youth-targeted interventions was clearly indicated by the 1994 Surgeon General's Report (p. 230), which noted that "in the absence of intervention, adolescent smokers [and smokeless tobacco users] will most likely become adult smokers." The report concluded that "most adolescent smokers are addicted to nicotine and report that they want to quit but are unable to do so; they experience relapse and withdrawal symptoms similar to those reported by adults" (p. 5). Moreover, a 1992 U.S. national survey of tobacco use by 12 to 17 year-olds found that, by age 17, approximately 50% of these children had already tried, and failed, to quit smoking, and that 38% of them would have at least some level of interest in youth-oriented cessation programs if such programs were offered (Gallup, 1992).

Interestingly, similar findings had been obtained 16 years earlier in a study conducted by the tobacco industry. The results of that study, titled "Project 16," were not voluntarily disclosed, but rather came to light during the course of the FDA's development of its proposal to regulate tobacco. In brief, Project 16 found that more than 50% of young smokers had tried to quit, and approximately two-thirds regretted having ever started smoking by age 17 (FDA, 1995; Kessler et al., 1996). These observations suggest that the problem of tobacco use among youth is a complex one involving various social and developmental pressures which put youth at high risk to initiate tobacco use, as well as at high risk for physiologically-based nicotine dependence.

Unfortunately, at present, there is little evidence of effective youth-targeted smoking cessation interventions (for an exception, see Myers, Brown, & Kelly, this publication). The 1994 Surgeon General's Report and the Institute of Medicine Report were able to summarize the state of the art in youth-targeted smoking cessation in just a few pages. The Surgeon General's Report findings concurred with those of the Institute of Medicine, which summarized the status of youth treatment as follows: "Few studies have been conducted on adolescent cessation of tobacco use, and those vary considerably in scientific quality; many are anecdotal. Therefore, at this time, no effective means are known for helping youths to quit using tobacco or to remain abstinent once they have attempted to quit" (p. 159).

CURRENT STATUS OF ADOLESCENT TOBACCO USE CESSATION RESEARCH

As introduced above, two major reviews of the literature on youth tobacco use by the Surgeon General and the Institute of Medicine have similarly concluded that: (1) little systematic research has been conducted; (2) the research that has been conducted has provided little evidence of effective treatment development; and (3) effective interventions are needed to prevent the transition from youthful smoking to adult smoking, disease and death. These reports based their findings on quasi-experimental and experimental work. Thus, only four or five studies were mentioned per report.

By not limiting the included studies to pure experiments only, researchers were able to conduct a review of 17 adolescent smoking cessation trials and 17 prevention trials that focused on regular adolescent tobacco use (Sussman, Lichtman, Ritt, & Pallonen, in press). The cessation studies centered on older adolescents, whereas the prevention studies focused on young adolescents.

Ten of the cessation studies used single-group designs, whereas all of the prevention studies used at least quasi-experimental designs. Of the cessation studies, an average of 62% of tobacco users participated in an initial smoking cessation session. Of those who attended a first session, an average of 78% were present at the last session and, of those at post-test, 90% were followed-up an average of six months later. Post-test cessation rates averaged 21%, whereas follow-up cessation rates averaged 13%.

Of the prevention studies, perhaps 80-90% of regular tobacco users participated in an initial cessation session, with an average attrition rate of 20% by the last session. Follow-up rates averaged 64% an average of 44 months after immediate post-test. "Cessation" rates averaged 5% in the prevention programs. Thus, prevention studies served 20% more tobacco users (70% versus 48%), followed-up approximately the same percentage of initial participants (45% versus 43%)–albeit over a much longer period of time–and obtained a somewhat lower mean cessation rate at follow-up (5% versus 13%). The cessation studies, therefore, appeared to be more effective than prevention studies in achieving sustained cessation. Nevertheless, the scientific status of cessation programming is far behind that of prevention programming. Unlike prevention research, no comparable set of finite theoretical camps have emerged, comparison groups are rarely used to evaluate treatment efficacy, corroborative reports (e.g., biochemical validation) are rarely employed, and data sets tend to be incomplete (only 11 of 17 cessation studies report retention and immediate post-test cessation rates). The authors concluded that there is hope in cessation research, but more advanced scientific work needs to be undertaken.

It should be mentioned that the naturally occurring quit rate among older adolescent tobacco users is approximately 8%, whereas the naturally occurring quit rate among young adolescents is approximately 3% (Sussman, Lichtman, Ritt, & Pallonen, in press). Thus, in comparison with naturally occurring quit rates, smoking cessation programs triple quit rates initially. However, by several months after a cessation program concludes, cessation rates fall only to twice that of naturally occurring quit rates. Among prevention programs, cessation rates are about twice the rate of naturally occurring quit rates.

The Sussman et al. review is encouraging with respect to the potential of research to yield improved tobacco prevention and cessation approaches. In fact, taken as a whole, the treatment studies in particular yielded cessation rates that are within the range of those achieved in some studies of adults (e.g., Shiffman, Mason & Henningfield, 1998; US DHHS, 1998; Abrams et al., 1996). Maintenance of participation in the cessation groups appears to be one important determinant of positive outcomes. Nonetheless, these studies leave unanswered fundamental questions such as how to establish and sustain motivated participation of youth in smoking cessation programs, as well as identify the apparent diversity of other determinants of success and failure.

Challenges in Adolescent Tobacco Cessation Research

The challenges to develop effective interventions for youth are considerable. The overwhelming majority of research on the pathogenesis, clinical symptoms, course, and treatment of tobacco addiction has been with adult cigarette smokers. Henningfield (1994, p. 96-97) concluded: "We need a pediatric-medicine approach whereby we build on the adult knowledge base and extend it to youth, discovering where there are differences." Whereas this conceptualization may seem straightforward, the challenges are considerable.

The foci of the remainder of this paper are six major challenges presented in tobacco use cessation research with adolescents. These are: (1) high levels of nicotine dependence can be achieved in adolescents; (2) difficulties in modifying social factors may inhibit quit attempts; (3) possibly weaker (relative to adults) health risk perceptions might inhibit quitting; (4) several adolescent-specific intrapersonal factors may inhibit quitting; (5) adapting adult cessation programming to adolescents is complicated by many lifestyle and developmental factors that distinguish youth from adults; and (6) adolescent-specific issues in the evaluation of medications.

Pediatric Nicotine Dependence

Many youth have a stronger level of nicotine dependence than is generally assumed in models which view youth tobacco use as largely determined by social pressures (see Kassel, this publication). The 1994 Surgeon General's Report and the 1994 Report of the Institute of Medicine (Lynch & Bonnie, 1994; US DHHS, 1994) both concluded that tobacco-using youth are at high risk of developing nicotine dependence, and that much stronger efforts need to be made to prevent tobacco use and treat those who are addicted. Some striking facts concerning the nature and scope of the problem underscore the high level of concern (Gallup, 1992; Riley, Woodard, Barienie, & Mabe, 1996; US DHHS, 1994; Food and Drug Administration, 1995; Centers for Disease Control and Prevention (CDC), 1994).

Youth who smoke daily show signs of nicotine withdrawal and dependence that is directly related to the number of cigarettes smoked per day. In fact, an analysis of data from the 1993 Teenage Attitudes and Practice Survey revealed a linear relation between number of cigarettes smoked per day and the likelihood of reporting that it "is really hard to quit" (CDC, 1994). Similarly, a recent analysis of predictors of smoking cessation in 12-18 year-old adolescents who were surveyed up to three times at one year intervals determined smoking cessation rates are an inverse function of smoking status at the initial assessment (Sargent, Mott, & Stevens, 1998). They found that the smoking cessation rates were 46.3% among occasional smokers, 12.3% among daily smokers of 1 to 9 cigarettes, and 6.8% among daily smokers of 10 or more cigarettes. Moreover, intent to quit smoking was only a reliable predictor of cessation among occasional smokers.

These consistent results confirm that young people do, indeed, become addicted to nicotine. Three recent reviews of nicotine medications have concluded that their use should be considered in young people who are unable to quit smoking (American Psychiatric Association (APA), 1996; Fiore et al., 1996; Henningfield, 1995; Patten, this publication). Unfortunately, as noted in these reviews, few data are available on the use of nicotine medications in adolescents that could provide guidance on adapting their use to youth populations.

Age of Onset of Tobacco Use

An important issue that supports the need for earlier interventions is that earlier onset of tobacco use may lead to higher ultimate levels of dependence (e.g., Chassin, Presson, Sherman & Edwards, 1990; Coambs, Li & Kozlowski, 1992). For example, Breslau and Peterson (1996) found that age of smoking onset was related to cessation difficulty; with potential confounders controlled for, the likelihood of cessation was significantly lower in smokers who initiated smoking before age 13 (Breslau & Peterson, 1996). Similarly, Stanton (1995) found that 18-year-olds were more likely to be dependent on tobacco (DSM-III-R criteria) if they reported becoming regular smokers before age 15 than from ages 16 to 18. It is increasingly accepted that public health efforts to delay smoking among adolescents might reduce cigarette consumption in early adulthood (Breslau, 1993). Moreover, it is generally assumed that the earlier the onset of use of an addicting drug (across a broad range of addictive drugs), and the more refractory the individuals are to treatment (Buydens-Branchey, Branchey, Noumair, 1989; Kandel & Yamaguchi, 1985; Robins & Przybeck, 1985).

This factor is not well understood because age of onset of tobacco use can be confounded with years of tobacco use and other variables in assessing predictors of treatment outcome. An examination of available literature reveals a less consistent and probably more complex picture than the foregoing generalizations would suggest. For example, definition of age of onset (i.e., any use, daily use, 100 cigarettes, etc.) varies across studies. Also, Hurtado and Conway (1996) found that age of smoking onset was not predictive of "policy-induced" cessation (i.e., restrictions on smoking) among new recruits to the U.S. Navy, but number of cigarettes per day and years of smoking were (Hurtado & Conway, 1996). Other studies have documented that adolescents can be exposed to significant levels of nicotine and show signs of dependence early in their smoking career (McNeill, 1991; Pechacek et al.,

1984; Prokhorov, Pallonen, Fava, Ding & Niaura, 1996), but most of these studies have not specifically evaluated age of onset as a factor in the dependence process in its own right. Clearly, much research remains to be done to elucidate the many factors that interact with age of onset of smoking.

Social Factors

Social factors that motivate smoking among adults are important determinants of the initiation of smoking in youth (US DHHS, 1994; Lynch and Bonnie, 1994). Social factors may be equally important in the cessation of smoking in youth. For example, social reasons to quit are mentioned relatively often in the literature on self-initiated adolescent tobacco use cessation, and include perceived peer and family influence (Chassin et al., 1991; see review in Sussman et al., in press). Conversely, those youth who report having friends who are smokers, and who report receiving a relatively greater number of cigarette offers, are less likely to quit. Perceived peer approval regarding smoking, or at least perceived peer tolerance regarding one's own behavior, is related to lower quit rates. Likewise, perceived parental tolerance of smoking, and relatively lower parental expectation regarding one's standard of behavior (e.g., school performance), are predictive of lower quit rates. It should also be noted that social factor may operate somewhat differently for boys versus girls (see Wagner & Atkins, this publication).

One may conjecture, however, that youth also experience weaker social motivational factors to quit than adults because their friends generally are not yet experiencing serious smoking-caused disease. Thus, even if youth are able to successfully negotiate a one-to-two week withdrawal period, they may relapse because their friends and family either smoke or do not provide a barrier to their own return to smoking. Potentially, during cessation, they may have received little praise or other social support for their quit attempts from others. However, much research remains to be done concerning social influences on smoking cessation among youth.

Health Risk Perceptions

Health effects are often reported as a reason for quitting tobacco use in retrospective reports or among tobacco users wanting to quit; regular smokers report less knowledge of the negative consequences of tobacco use than do same-age nonsmokers (Sussman et al., in press; US DHHS, 1994), and quitters hold more negative beliefs than current smokers about the psychological and health consequences of smoking (Chassin et al., 1991). In addition, nonsmokers from high-risk groups are less likely to be smokers if their best friend is not a smoker, and if they place a high value on health (Sussman et al., 1993). Cohn, Macfarlane, Yanez and Imai (1995) found that adolescents are concerned about their health but feel less optimistic about avoiding disease and injury than adults. Perhaps an intervention emphasizing the value of health and optimism about avoiding disease would assist adolescent prevention and cessation efforts. Unfortunately, concern about personal health risks is not readily accepted by cigarette smoking youth–or at least is not effectively translated into effective therapies. Youth do have health concerns that are similar in many respects to those of adults (Cohn et al., 1995), but it is likely that they will need "youth-customized" messages to translate these concerns into sources of active motivation to achieve and sustain abstinence.

As another case in point, tobacco marketers have capitalized upon the mixed perceptions by youth and mixed messages by some public health professionals about smoking. In particular, smokeless tobacco marketing efforts stressed the relative healthfulness of their products compared to cigarettes (e.g., the "reach for a pouch instead of a puff" advertising campaigns of the 1980s) (Connolly, 1995; Henningfield, Fant & Tomar, 1997). These marketing programs have gone to great lengths to associate their products with activities and people who embody extraordinary physical prowess, such as baseball players, rodeo stars, and other athletes. In the past, even some public health professionals and researchers advocated smokeless tobacco as a better alternative to cigarettes for people who could not give up tobacco altogether (Rodu, 1994; Russell, Jarvis & Feyerband, 1980). However, the current availability of pure nicotine medications makes such advice inappropriate (Greene, 1997). It was not until after the 1986 Report of the Surgeon General that U.S. public health agencies began to voice unequivocal assertions about the harm of both smoked and smokeless tobacco products. One of the lessons learned is that marketing and labeling approaches emphasizing the relative benefits of nicotine medications or nicotine-containing products need to be especially sensitive to the tendency of young people to misinterpret "safer" as "safe." A stronger base of research on the risk/benefit perceptions of youth would appear essential to enabling more effective efforts to promote and support youth cessation activity.

Intrapersonal Factors

Relatively unexplored motivational factors may represent potential impediments to achieving and sustaining cessation among adolescents (Aubrey, 1996; Pallonen et al., 1998; Sussman, 1996). Adolescent smokers who agree that society has the right to take action on the smoking problem, who report disapproval of tobacco industry advertising, or who question the appropriateness of their own tobacco use, are relatively likely to be motivated to quit (Sussman et al., in press). Substantial work is needed to identify both the energy and direction components of motivating adolescent tobacco users to cease use (Nezami and Sussman, under review). Direction components would identify discrepancies between the adolescent's current and desired behavior and self-perceptions. The potential to resolve such discrepancies by quitting tobacco use has been a laudable goal of recent efforts. In addition, youth must feel that they have the energy to sustain a quit attempt, which entails that their current skills match the capacities of successful quitters.

Another group of important intrapersonal factors includes risk-taking, lack of belief in law abidance, and lack of bonding to organized activities in the community. Preference or predisposition toward risk-taking and related variables are major predictors of continued smoking and lowered rates of quitting (e.g., Laoye, Creswell, and Stone, 1972; Skinner et al., 1985; Stewart and Livson, 1963; Sussman et al., in press). Risk-taking or sensation seeking may be relatively stable traits, and are difficult to modify through a brief intervention. Such characteristics are great impediments to smoking cessation, especially as tobacco use becomes increasingly associated with a rebel lifestyle. Tobacco cessation strategies will need to address adolescents' tendencies toward rebelliousness, either by providing alternative options (Sussman, 1996), through program messages (Palmgreen et al., 1995) or through instruction on non-rebellious means to cope with subjective stress or lack of excitement.

Generalizability of Adult Tobacco Treatment Strategies

Much work needs to be done to identify the factors that determine which young people will attempt to quit smoking and, among these, who will be in greatest need of assistance (Rose, Chassin, Presson & Sherman, 1996). Effective interventions for adults (e.g., use of a diary, planning a quit date, nicotine medications) have not been adapted and applied to young people in a systematic manner. This lack of application is not surprising, given marked differences in lifestyle characteristics between adults and youth. The adolescent stage of development is characterized by a struggle to define and enhance personal identity. Typically, adolescents do not carry appointment books, do not have the responsibility of taking care of others, and do not plan a great deal for future events. Thus, one might expect that various planning, analytical, and social support components of adult cessation programs will not be generalizable to youth. Possibly, youth cessation programs demand more structure and guidance from a trained facilitator. They may need relatively frequent reminders regarding why they are quitting as well as how to quit.

Preliminary data from Prokhorov et al. (1996) suggest that approximately 20% of young cigarette smokers (mean age 17 years) are at high levels of nicotine dependence (i.e., score 6 or greater on a modified Fagerstrom Questionnaire). Thus, some percentage of youth might benefit from use of medications approved for use in adults (Fiore et al., 1996; Henningfield, 1995;

Patten, this publication). However, because this preliminary study was conducted among vocational-technical students who are at higher risk for early smoking initiation/high smoking intensity compared with same-age students enrolled in academic programs, such data need to be collected from a broader sample of American youth.

How to maintain program effects beyond the initial quit attempt seems to be of paramount importance. Apparently, while 21% of youth will quit in a clinic context, 8% of these persons relapse by six months post-treatment (Sussman, Lichtman, Ritt & Pallonen, in press). Thus youth show at best half the cessation rate achieved by adults. They may not, for example, have much of a support system to help them remain smoke-free. Without social barriers, implicit cognition processes may steer adolescents back in the direction of using (Stacy, 1995). Other variables such as comorbid conditions (e.g., depression, other substance abuse) may inhibit cessation efforts to the extent that nicotine is being for self-medication (Brown, Lewinsohn, Seeley, & Wagner, 1996). It is not clear to what extent comorbid conditions play a greater or lesser role for youth as compared to adults. Clearly, maintenance of cessation is a most important issue to address in future research.

Medication-Specific Research Issues and Questions

It has been suggested that, because some youth appear to be at high levels of nicotine dependence, they should be considered potential candidates for nicotine medication therapy (Prokhorov et al., 1996). Others have provided general guidance for the use of medications in young people, but with acknowledgement that there are few data supporting diagnostic and dosing procedures for nicotine dependence among youth (Fiore et al., 1996; Henningfield, 1995; Kassel, this publication; Patten, this publication). The over-the-counter nicotine gum and patch products are specifically labeled (as stipulated by the FDA) to prohibit purchase by persons under 18 years of age, and such persons are advised to see their doctor if they are considering use of the products.

Youth, like adults, report many reasons for their tobacco use that are related to the potential pharmacological effects of nicotine. Available evidence suggests general similarities in the clinical manifestation of nicotine dependence in youth and in adults (Sussman et al., in press). However, it is plausible that all symptoms are not identical, and that the significance of certain symptoms may vary by age. It is also often difficult to determine the degree to which such effects are secondary to the dependence process (e.g., perceived performance or mood control benefits of nicotine may largely reflect reversal of withdrawal symptoms) versus reflect direct actions of nicotine itself (e.g., weight control appears to be a direct effect of nicotine that can result in lower growth-associated weight gain in nicotine users compared to non-users).

Interestingly, the R.J. Reynolds Tobacco Company, and tobacco industry-supported researchers such as Warburton, claim that the direct beneficial pharmacologic effects of nicotine–not its reinforcing and physiological dependence-producing effects–are the main reasons for tobacco use (Robinson & Pritchard, 1992; Warburton, 1988). The process factors which may inhibit or speed the transition from initial use to addiction have not been studied well outside the tobacco industry, but may include a range of effects of nicotine which at least some tobacco users contribute to their physical dependence on nicotine (US DHHS, 1988).

It is possible that an over-the-counter drug product could be part of the treatment options for youth with nicotine addiction, and in turn could lower the prevalence of tobacco use among youth. Unfortunately, there are little data upon which to empirically base estimates of safety or efficacy of OTC remedies for children. A pilot study by Smith et al. (1996) suggests that transdermal nicotine, when used with youth, does not produce untoward side effects significantly different in degree or quality than those observed in similar studies with adults. However, this study was not intended to evaluate efficacy, elucidate factors related to efficacy, or determine general safety.

Of youth who would seem to be the most likely candidates for nicotine medication therapy (the ones with higher levels of nicotine dependence), it is not clear what percentage would be deterred from using the medications by financial pressures or social factors (e.g., lack of parent's approval). Moreover, one of the principle designers of nicotine gum, Ove Ferno, specifically proposed placing nicotine in a gum formulation that would not be particularly appealing to chew, except for its medicinal effect, as a barrier to inappropriate use by children (Ferno, 1973; personal communication from Dr. Ove Ferno). While such gum formulations provide barriers to misuse by children, they also present the possibility that the medication would not be used effectively in adolescents.

The rational basis for using adult-tested medications in youth, and the complications in studying such applications are not unique to tobacco dependence treatment products. In the fall of 1997, the FDA proposed a regulation that would require the evaluation of many medicines for pediatric populations. The agency noted that one challenge faced by the pharmaceutical industry is the modification of drug formulations to make them more appealing to youth (Federal Register, 1997; College on Problems of Drug Dependence (CPDD), 1998). This process is particularly complicated with respect to nicotine medications because of the concerns that more appealing flavors have the potential to increase inappropriate use and dependence among youth. This occurred with moist snuff products that were developed as "starter" products (Connolly, 1995; Henningfield, Radzius & Cone, 1995; FDA, 1995). Finally, many otherwise appropriate young candidates for nicotine medications might be discouraged by health professionals who are skeptical of the need for and probable success of medications.

Specific Research Questions

There are remarkably few data on any aspect of the safety, toxicity, kinetics, abuse liability or treatment efficacy of any nicotine medications in youth (see Patten, this publication). The absence of such data makes it difficult to determine if there is a generally favorable risk/benefit ratio for the use of such products to treat nicotine dependence among young people. The risk of pediatric research and concerns raised by Institutional Review Boards about testing young people (in the absence of a clear statement of public health need) may have served as barriers to such research in the past.

It is unclear which of the several putative medications would be most appropriate for initial consideration in youth treatment efforts. For instance, it could be argued that nicotine transdermal systems would offer low risk to young people due to the almost complete separation of the behavior of self-administration from the pharmacologic effects of nicotine. In addition, the mild psychoactivity and perturbation of mood that can accompany gum use should be less with the patch (Henningfield & Keenan, 1993). On the other hand, the gum already has a remarkable record of low abuse and toxicity incidence and some ability to provide a rapid response to needs and cravings which may be important for youth as it is for many adults (e.g., Shiffman et al., 1998).

A nicotine nasal spray and vapor inhaler also are available by prescription (Hurt et al., 1998; Schneider et al., 1995; Schneider et al., 1996). These products, while having a low abuse potential relative to cigarettes, might be of greater concern for youth because of pharmacological and sensory aspects that might increase their potential for youth abuse (Leischow, 1994; Schuh, Henningfield & Stitzer, 1997). Furthermore, there are many fewer clinical data for these products than exist for nicotine gum and patch. Nonetheless, these medications may offer important and heretofore unidentified advantages for application to youth. Finally, another prescription smoking cessation aid, the antidepressant bupropion, is effective for adults but has not been evaluated in youth.

Several more fundamental questions remain: (1) Are the kinetics of nicotine from nicotine medications the same for adolescents as for adults? (2) Are presently documented untoward effects and limitations of medications the same in youth as in adults (e.g., "chewing" compliance with gum)? (3) Are specific beneficial effects of medications the same in adolescents as in adults (e.g., reduction of withdrawal with gum and patch and reduction of weight gain with gum)? (4) Are there abuse liability concerns with youth that are not significant for adults? (5) Is using nicotine medication longer than indicated of greater concern among young people than in adults? (6) How should medication tapering and discontinuation be accomplished? (7) How do young people compare to adults in their nicotine dosage needs? (8) Are pharmacologic adjunct dose-determining questions such as number of cigarettes smoked per day adequate for young populations? (9) Are there new diagnostic/dosing questions that might be useful with adolescent populations? (10) Do any of the variations of the Fagerstrom Tolerance Questionnaire provide an adequate basis for dose determination (Kassel, this publication; Prokhorov et al., 1996; Heatherton et al., 1991) in youth?

Important research queries pertaining to behavioral determinants of success in treatments for youth are alluded to by recent reviews of how to integrate behavioral and pharmacological treatment approaches (Cinciripini & McClure, 1998; Shiffman et al., 1998). Specific questions pertaining to youth include the following: (1) What is the best form of ancillary treatment for those individuals using medication? (2) What types of information needs to be conveyed to youth about the use of medications and how will the information be conveyed? (3) What types of support materials are necessary to enhance compliance and facilitate cessation? (4) How will the advertising of medications to youth change their attitudes and concerns (or lack thereof) about tobacco dependence? (5) How could youth treatment be most effectively integrated with youth prevention programs so that youth whose tobacco use has progressed beyond social experimentation could be triaged into appropriate treatment? (6) How should cultural differences be taken into account in cessation and prevention programs?

Finally, persons under 18 years of age constitute an enormously heterogeneous assembly of individuals. This implies that the appropriateness of specific behavioral support programs may vary from youth to youth. Insight here may be provided by the increasingly well appreciated concept that treatment approaches should be tailored to the stage of readiness to quit smoking to maximize compliance with the effort (Prochaska et al., 1993). However, this stage of change model is another example of a model well researched with adults (Prochaska & Velicer, 1996; Farkas et al., 1996; Pierce, Farkas & Giplin, 1998) but relatively unresearched with youth.

CONCLUSIONS

Pediatric nicotine dependence is a substantial and important public health problem. The successful reduction of smoking among youth in the 1970s and early 1980s proved the potential effectiveness of prevention approaches (Sussman et al., 1995). However, prevention is not enough as many youth continue to develop nicotine dependence. As former FDA Commissioner David A. Kessler has observed: "By altering the smoking habits of young people, we could radically reduce the incidence of smoking-related death and disease, and the next generation would see nicotine addiction go the way of smallpox and poliomyelitis." Although the challenges in developing effective interventions for youth are considerable, they are more than matched by the potential benefit to public health.

Unfortunately, developing effective interventions to treat adolescent tobacco dependence is a daunting task. This is evidenced by the discouraging conclusions of the 1994 Surgeon General's and Institute of Medicine's Reports discussed in this paper (US DHHS, 1994; Lynch & Bonnie, 1994). The issues are diverse, and range from basic questions regarding the etiology of nicotine dependence and the need for validated instruments to diagnose dependence in youth, to the need for clinical pharmacology studies on the kinetics of nicotine delivered to young people. Adult tobacco users are very likely to be addicted and therefore have a high probability of continuing to use tobacco for many years if they are not treated. Young people, however, often have not yet stabilized their tobacco use, and many may be on a trajectory that could lead to either dependence or cessation in the near term. We do not know enough about this trajectory to assess indicators or predictors of outcomes, nor do we know enough about the rate of development of the trajectory. One theoretical concern is that the provision of medication to young people earlier on the trajectory is that it may expose them to risks (e.g., seizures from bupropion, or developing dependence to nicotine) when these young people would have actually stopped smoking on their own.

Developing and evaluating tobacco dependence treatment approaches for youth will require a broader application of experimental study designs, which include collecting a broader range of types of data than have been typical to date (see Sussman, Lichtman, Ritt & Pallonen, in press). More comprehensive theoretical development also is needed to address the range of social, intrapersonal, health belief, and pharmacological factors that are likely determinants of treatment outcome. Also, better implementation and follow-up data are needed. For example, more data are needed to calculate the reach of cessation programming (how many will attend a cessation program of those notified). Data should be gathered on the percent reduction in tobacco use among non-quitters, because available data suggest that some youth who do not quit do decrease the amount of tobacco they use (Sussman, Lichtman, Ritt & Pallonen, in press). Whether such effects are sustained, and/or lead to increased subsequent cessation attempts also needs to be assessed.

Treatment of adolescent smokers will likely require specific matching of intervention approach to level of use and dependence as well as to the level and nature of placement in school and non-school settings. It appears plausible that interventions similar to those targeted at adults should be used with older teens (16-17 years old) who have been smoking regularly for over a year and who consume over 10 cigarettes per day. Such individuals may benefit from nicotine replacement therapy, but there are woefully few data to guide such generalized application. Thus, such use should be guided with advice of an appropriate health care professional. Other interventions that focus on younger smokers and those who have not been smoking as long also need to be developed. Finally, developmentally sensitive treatment strategies, which take into account adolescent lifestyle factors, comorbid conditions, and cognitive tendencies, will need to be developed. The research challenges posed here are many and diverse, but all of the issues raised in this review could be addressed by concerted research efforts. The opportunity to reduce the current projections of premature tobacco-caused mortality in one-third to one-half of cigarette smoking youth strongly argue for such efforts.

REFERENCES

Abrams, D.B., Orleans, T.C., Niaura, R.S., Goldstein, M.G., Prochaska, J.O., & Velicer, W. (1996). Integrating individual and public health perspectives for treatment of tobacco dependence under managed health care: a combined stepped-care and matching model. *Annals of Behavioral Medicine, 18*(4), 290-304.

American Psychiatric Association (APA). (1996). Practice guideline for the treatment of patients with nicotine dependence. *American Journal of Psychiatry, 153*(suppl), 1-31.

Aubrey, L.L. (1996). Motivational enhancement therapy (MET) for adolescent substance abusers. *Paper presentation for the Tobacco Cessation Project for Youth,* AMA-CDC, Chicago.

Breslau, N. Daily cigarette consumption in early adulthood: age of smoking initiation and duration of smoking. (1993). *Drug and Alcohol Dependence, 33,* 287-291.

Breslau, N. & Peterson, E. (1996). Smoking cessation in young adults: age at initiation of smoking and other suspected influences. *American Journal of Health, 86,* 214-220.

Brown, R.A., Lewinsohn, P.M., Seeley, J.R., & Wagner, E.F. (1996). Cigarette smoking, major depression, and other psychiatric disorders among adolescents. *Journal of the American Academy of Child and Adolescent Psychiatry, 35,* 1602-1610.

Buydens-Branchey, L., Branchey, M.H., & Noumair, D. (1989) Age of alcoholism onset: Relationship to psychopathy. *Archives of General Psychiatry, 46,* 225-230.

Centers for Disease Control and Prevention. (1993). Cigarette smoking attributable to mortality and years of potential life lost-United Sates, 1990. *Morbidity and Mortality Weekly Report, 42,* 37-39.

Centers for Disease Control and Prevention. (April 1998). Tobacco use among high school students-United States, 1997. *Morbidity and Mortality Weekly Report, 45*(12), 229-233.

Centers for Disease Control and Prevention. (October 21, 1994). Reasons for tobacco use and symptoms of nicotine withdrawal among adolescent and young adult tobacco users-United States, 1993. *Morbidity and Mortality Weekly Report, 43*(41), 745-750.

Chassin, L., Presson, C.C., Sherman, S.J., & Edwards, D.A. (1990). The natural history of cigarette smoking: Predicting young-adult smoking outcomes from adolescent smoking patterns. *Health Psychology*, 9(6), 701-716.

Cinciripini, P.M., & McClure, J.B. (1998). Smoking cessation: recent developments in behavioral and pharmacologic interventions. *Oncology*, 12(2), 249-259.

Coambs, R.B., Li, S., & Kozlowski, L.T. (1992). Age interacts with heaviness of smoking in predicting success in cessation of smoking. *American Journal of Epidemiology*, 135, 240-246.

Cohn, L.D., Macfarlane, S., Yanez, C., & Imai, W.K. (1995). Risk Perception: Differences Between Adolescents and Adults. *Health Psychology*, 14(3), 217-222.

College on Problems of Drug Dependence. (February 25, 1998). Comment on "Regulations requiring manufacturers to assess the safety and effectiveness of new drugs and biological products in pediatric patients." *Department of Health and Human Services. Food and Drug Administration, 21* CFR Parts 201, 312, 314, and 601.

Connolly, G.N. (1995). The marketing of nicotine addiction by one oral snuff manufacturer. *Tobacco Control, 4*, 73-79.

Connolly, G.N., Winn, D.M., Hecht, S.S., Henningfield, J.E., Walker, B., & Hoffmann, D. (1986). The reemergence of smokeless tobacco. *The New England Journal of Medicine, 314*, 1020-1027.

Farkas, A.J., Peirce, J.P., Zhu, S.H., Rosbrook, B., Gilpin, E.A., Berry, C., & Kaplan, R.M. (1996). Addiction versus stages of change models in predicting smoking cessation. *Addiction, 91*(9), 1271-1280.

Ferno, O. (1973). A substitute for tobacco smoking. *Pyschopharmacologia, 31*, 201-204.

Federal Register. (August 15, 1997). Regulations requiring manufacturers to assess the safety and effectiveness of new biological products in pediatric patients; Proposed rule. *Federal Register, Vol 62*, FR43899.

Food and drug Administration. (August 11, 1995). Regulations restricting the sale and distribution of cigarettes and smokeless tobacco products to protect children and adolescents. Proposed rule. *Federal Register, 21 CFR Part 801* et al., pp.41314-41787.

Food and Drug Administration. (August 28, 1996). Regulations restricting the sale and distribution of cigarettes and smokeless tobacco products to protect children and adolescents. Final rule. *Federal Register, 21 CFR, Part 801* et al., pp.44396-45318.

Fiore, M., Bailey, W.C., Cohen, S.J., Dorfman, S.F., Goldstein, M.G., Gritz, E.R., Heymen, R.B., Holbrook, J., Jaen, C.R., Kottke, T.E., Lando, H.A., Mecklenburg, R., Mullen, P.D., Nett, L.M., Robinson, L., Stitzer, M.L., Tommasello, A.C., Vilejo, L., & Wewers, M.E. (April 1996). Smoking Cessation. Clinical Practice Guideline, No. 18. US DHHS, *Agency for Health Care Policy and Research*, Rockville, MD, AHCPR Publication No. 96-0692. April 1996.

George G. Gallup International Institute. (September 1992). Teen-Age Attitudes and Behavior Concerning Tobacco. Report of the Findings. Princeton, NJ.

Gerlach, K.K., Cummings, M., Hyland, A., Giplin, E.A., Johnson, M.D., Pierce, J.P. (1998). Trends in cigar consumption and smoking prevalence. Cigars: Health effects and trends. *Smoking and Tobacco Control Monograph 9, National Cancer Institute*, (pp. 21-53). NIH Publication No. 98-4302.

Greene, J.C. (1997). Summary and conclusion. *Advances in Dental Research, 11*(3), 350-353.

Heatherton, T.F., Kozlowski, L.T., Frecker, R.C., & Fagerstrom, K.O. (1991). The

Fagerstrom Test for nicotine dependence: A revision of the Fagerstrom Tolerance Questionnaire. *British Journal of Addiction, 86,* 1119-1127.

Henningfield, J.E. (1994). Nicotine addiction. *A report of the second Ross Roundtable on Critical Issues on Family Medicine,* pp. 96-97.

Henningfield, J.E. (1995). Nicotine medications for smoking cessation. *New England Journal of Medicine, 333,* 1196-1203.

Henningfield, J.E., Clayton, R., Pollin, W. (1990). The involvement of tobacco in alcoholism and illicit drug use. *British Journal of Addiction, 85,* 279-292.

Henningfield, J.E. & Keenan, R.M. (1993). Nicotine delivery kinetics and abuse liability. *Journal of Consulting and Clinical Psychology, 61*(5), 743-750.

Henningfield, J.E., Radzius, A., Cone, E.J. (1995). Estimation of available nicotine content of six smokeless tobacco products. *Tobacco Control, 4*(1), 57-61.

Henningfield, J.E. & Slade, J. (1998). Tobacco-dependence medications: Public health and regulatory issues. *Food and Drug Law Journal, 53*(suppl), 75-114.

Hurt, R.D., Dale, L.C., Croghan, I.T., Gomez-Dahl, L.C., Offord, K.P. (1998). Nicotine nasal spray for smoking cessation: Pattern of use, side effects, relief of withdrawal symptoms, and cotinine levels. *Mayo Clinic Proceedings, 73,* 118-125.

Hurtado, L.S. & Conway, L.T. (1996). Changes in smoking prevalence following a strict no-smoking policy in US Navy recruit training. *Military Medicine, 161,* 571-576.

Johns Hopkins University School of Medicine, Society for Research on Nicotine and Tobacco. (Autumn 1995). Smoking Cessation: Alternative strategies. Proceedings of a national conference convened by the Behavioral Biology Research Center at Johns Hopkins University School of Medicine and the Society for Research on Nicotine and Tobacco (April 10-11, 1195, Washington DC). *Tobacco Control, supplement 2.*

Kandel, D.B. & Yamaguchi, K. (1985). Developmental patterns of the use of legal, illegal, and medically prescribed psychotropic drugs from adolescence to young adulthood. *Etiology of Drug Abuse: Implications for Prevention. NIDA Research Monograph, No. 56.* Rockville, MD: National Institute on Drug Abuse, DHHS Publication No. (ADM)87-1335, pp. 193-235.

Kessler, D.A. (1995). Nicotine addiction in young people. *New England Journal of Medicine, 333(3),* 186-189.

Kessler, D.A., Nantanblut, S.L., Wilkendfeld, J.P., Lorraine, C.C., Mayl, S.L., Bernstein, I.B.G., Thompson, L. (1996a). Nicotine addiction: A pediatric disease. *New England Journal of Medicine, 335,* 931-937.

Kessler, D.A., Witt, A., Barnett, P.S., Zeller, M.R., Nantanblut, S.L., Wilkenfeld, J.P., Lorraine, C.C., Thompson, L.J., Schultz, W.B. (1996b). The Food and Drug Administration's regulation of tobacco products. *New England Journal of Medicine, 335*(13), 988-994.

Laoye, J.A., Creswell, W., Stone, E.B. (1972). A cohort of 12,205 secondary school smokers. *Journal of School Health, 42,* 47-52.

Leischow, S.J. (1994). The nicotine vaporizer. *Health Values, 18*(3), 4-9.

Lynch, B. & Bonnie, R. (1994). *Growing Up Tobacco Free. Preventing Nicotine Addiction in Children and Youths.* Committee on Preventing Nicotine Addiction in Children and Youths, Division of Biobehavioral Sciences and Mental Disorders, Institute of Medicine. Washington DC: National Academy Press.

McNeill, A. (1991). The development of dependence on smoking in children. *British Journal of Addiction, 86,* 589-592.

Nezami, E. & Sussman, S. Motivation in tobacco use cessation research. Under review.

Pallonen, U.E., Velicer, W.F., Prochaska, J.O., Rossi, J.S., Bellis, J.M., Tsoh, J.Y., Migneault, J.P., Smith, N.F., Prokhorov, A.V. (1998). Computer-based smoking cessation interventions in adolescents: Description, feasibility, and six-month follow-up findings. *Substance Use and Misuse, 33,* 1-31.

Palmgreen, P., Lorch, E.P., Donohew, L., Harrington, N.G., Dsilva, M., Helm, D. (1995). Reaching at-risk populations in a mass media drug abuse prevention campaign: Sensation seeking as a targeting variable. *Drugs and Society, 8,* 29-45.

Pechacek, T.F., Murray, D.M., Luepkar, R.V., Mittelmark, M.B., Johnson, C.A., Shutz, J.M. (1984). Measurement of adolescent smoking behavior: Rationale and methods. *Journal of Behavioral Medicine, 7,* 123-140.

Peto, R., Lopez, A.D., Boreham, J., Thun, M., Heath Jr., C. (1994). Mortality From Smoking in Developed Countries, 1950-2000. Indirect Estimates from National Vital Statistics. Oxford University Press.

Pierce, J.P., Farkas, A.J., Gilpin, E.A. (1998). Beyond stages of change: The quitting continuum measures progress towards successful smoking cessation. *Addiction, 93*(2), 277-286.

Pierce, J.P. & Gilpin, E.A. (1996). How Long Will Today's New Adolescent Smoker Be Addicted to Cigarettes? *American Journal of Public Health, 86,* 253-256.

Prochaska, J.O., DiClimente, C.C., Velicer, W.F., Rossi, J.S. (1993). Standardized, individualized, interactive and personalized self-help programs for smoking cessation. *Health Psychology, 12*(5), 399-405.

Prochaska, J.O., Velicer, W.F. (1996). Comments on Farkas et al.'s "Addiction versus stages of change models in predicting smoking cessation." *Addiction, 91*(9), 1281-1292.

Prokhorov, A.V., Pallonen, U.V., Fava, J.L., Ding, L., Niaura, R. (1996). Measuring Nicotine Dependence Among High-Risk Adolescent Smokers. *Addictive Behaviors, 21*(1), 117-127.

Riley, W.T., Woodard, C.T., Barienei, J.T., Mabe, P.A. (1996). Perceived Smokeless Tobacco Addiction Among Adolescents. *Health Psychology, 15*(4), 289-292.

Robins, L.N. & Przybeck, T.R. (1985). Age of onset of drug use as a factor in drug and other disorders. *Etiology of drug abuse: Implications for prevention, NIDA Research Monograph, No.56.* Rockville, MD: National Institute on Drug Abuse. DHHS Publication No. (ADM)87-1335, pp.178-192.

Robinson, J.H. & Prithcard, W.S. (1992). The role of nicotine in tobacco use. *Psychopharmacology, 108,* 397-407.

Rodu, B. (1994). Editorial: An alternative approach to smoking control. *The American Journal of Medical Sciences, 308*(1), 32-34.

Rose, J.S., Chassin, L., Presson, C.C., Sherman, S.J. (1996). Prospective Predictors of Quit Attempts and Smoking Cessation in Young Adults. *Health Psychology, 15*(4), 261-268.

Russell, M.A.H., Jarvis, M.J., Feyerband, C. (1980). A new age for snuff? *The Lancet, March 1,* 474-475.

Sargent, J.D., Mott, L.A., Stevens, M. (1998). Predictors of smoking cessation in adolescents. *Archives of Pediatric Adolescent Medicine, 152*, 388-393.

Schneider, N.G., Olmstead, R., Mody, F.V., Doan, K., Franzon, M., Jarvik, M.E., Steinberg, C. (1995). Efficacy of a nicotine nasal spray in smoking cessation: A placebo-controlled, double-blind trial. *Addiction*, 90, 1671-1682.

Schneider, N.G., Olmstead, R., Nilsson, F., Mody, F.V., Franzon, M., Doan. K. (1996) Efficacy of a nicotine inhaler in smoking cessation: A double-blind, placebo controlled trial. *Addiction, 91*(9), 1293-1306.

Schuh, K.J., Schuh, L.M., Henningfield, J.E., Stitzer, M.L. (1997). Nicotine nasal spray and vapor inhaler: Abuse liability assessment. *Psychopharmacology, 130*, 352-361.

Shiffman, S., Mason, K.M., Henningfield, J.E. (1998). Tobacco dependence treatments: Review and prospectus. *Annual Reviews of Public Health, 19*, 335-358.

Skinner, W.F., Massey, J.L., Krohn, M.D., Lauer, R.M. (1985). Social influences and constraints in the initiation and cessation of adolescent tobacco use. *Journal of Behavioral Medicine, 8*, 353-376.

Slade, J. (1995). Are Tobacco Products Drugs? Evidence from US Tobacco. *Tobacco Control, 4*(1), 1-2.

Smith, T.A., House, R.F., Croghan, I.T., Gauvin, T.R., Colligan, R.C., Offord, K.P., Gomez-Dahl, L.C., Hurt, R.D. (1996). Nicotine Patch Therapy in Adolescent Smokers. *Pediatrics, 98*(4), 659-667.

Stacy, A.W. (1995). Memory association and ambiguous cues in models of alcohol and marijuana use. *Experimental and Clinical Psychopharmacology, 3*, 183-194.

Stanton, R.W. (1995). DSM-III-R Tobacco dependence and quitting during late adolescence. *Addictive Behaviors, 20*, 595-603.

Stewart, L., Livson, N. (1966). Smoking and rebelliousness: A longitudinal study from childhood to maturity. *Journal of Consulting Psychology, 30*, 225-229.

Sussman, S. (1996). Development of a drug abuse prevention curriculum for high risk youth. *Journal of Psychoactive Drugs, 28*, 169-182.

Sussman, Dent, C.W., Burton, D., Stacy, A.W., Flay, B.R. (1995). Developing school-based tobacco use prevention and cessation programs. Thousand Oaks, CA: Sage.

Sussman, S., Dent, C.W., Severson, H., Burton, D., Flay, B.R. (In press). Self-initiated quitting among adolescent smokers. *Preventive Medicine*.

Sussman, S., Dent, C.W., Stacy, A.W., Burton, D., Flay, B.R. (1993). Identification of which high risk youth smoke cigarettes regularly. *Health Values, 17*, 42-53.

Sussman, S., Lichtman, K., Ritt, A., Pallonen, U. (In press). Effects of thirty four adolescent tobacco use cessation and prevention trials on regular users of tobacco products. *Substance Use and Misuse*.

US Department of Health and Human Services. (1988). *The health consequences of smoking: Nicotine addiction. A Report of the Surgeon General*. Rockville, MD: US Department of Health and Human Services, Public Health Service, Centers for Disease Control, Office on Smoking and Health. DHS Publication No. (CDC) 88-8406.

US Department of Health and Human Services. (1994). *Preventing Tobacco Use Among Young People. A Report of the Surgeon General*. Atlanta, Georgia: US

Department of Health and Human Services, Public Health Service, Centers for Disease Control and Prevention, Office on Smoking and Health.

US Department of Health and Human Services. (1998). Tobacco use among U.S. racial/ethnic groups-African Americans, American Indians and Alaska Natives, Asian Americans and Pacific Islanders, and Hispanics: A Report of the Surgeon General. Atlanta, Georgia: US Department of Health and Human Services, Public Health Service, Centers for Disease Control and prevention, National Center for Chronic Disease Prevention and Health promotion, Office on Smoking and Health.

Warburton, D.M. (1988). The Puzzle of Nicotine Use. In Lader, M.H. (ed) *The Psychopharmacology of Addiction*. New York: Oxford University Press, pp. 27-49.

Are Adolescent Smokers Addicted to Nicotine? The Suitability of the Nicotine Dependence Construct as Applied to Adolescents

Jon D. Kassel

SUMMARY. Adolescent cigarette smoking has long been regarded as a major public health problem. Particularly disconcerting is the observation that over the last several years, greater numbers of adolescents are taking up this destructive behavior. While some have assumed that the majority of these smokers are, or will become, nicotine dependent, the fact is that we know very little about the phenomenon of nicotine dependence in adolescence. In this paper, the author reviews the theoretical and empirical bases from which inferences regarding addictive smoking in adolescence can be drawn. It appears that although a significant proportion of teenage smokers do progress to dependence, this is not an inevitable outcome for all adolescent smokers. Moreover, the scientific study of nicotine dependence among adolescents is still in its infancy and, as such, more work in the area of measurement and assessment needs to be done. Implications for prevention and intervention efforts are also discussed. *[Article copies available for a fee from The Haworth Docu-*

Jon D. Kassel, PhD, is affiliated with the University of Illinois at Chicago, Department of Psychology.

Address correspondence to Jon D. Kassel, PhD, University of Illinois at Chicago, Department of Psychology (MC 285), 1007 W. Harrison St., Chicago, IL 60607-7137 (E-mail: jkassel@uic.edu).

The writing of this article was supported, in part, by grant 1R29AA12240-01 from the National Institute on Alcohol Abuse and Alcoholism.

[Haworth co-indexing entry note]: "Are Adolescent Smokers Addicted to Nicotine? The Suitability of the Nicotine Dependence Construct as Applied to Adolescents." Kassel, Jon, D. Co-published simultaneously in *Journal of Child & Adolescent Substance Abuse* (The Haworth Press, Inc.) Vol. 9, No. 4, 2000, pp. 27-49; and: *Nicotine Addiction Among Adolescents* (ed: Eric F. Wagner) The Haworth Press, Inc., 2000, pp. 27-49. Single or multiple copies of this article are available for a fee from The Haworth Document Delivery Service [1-800-342-9678, 9:00 a.m. - 5:00 p.m. (EST). E-mail address: getinfo@haworthpressinc.com].

ment Delivery Service: 1-800-342-9678. E-mail address: <getinfo@haworthpres-sinc. com> Website: <http://www.haworthpressinc.com>]

KEYWORDS. Adolescence, smokers, nicotine dependence

Cigarette smoking remains the most preventable cause of morbidity and mortality in the United States today (U.S. Surgeon General, 1989, 1994). Well over 400,000 people die each year from smoking-related deaths (McGinnis & Foege, 1993). Since the first appearance of the widely publicized Surgeon General's report of 1964, there has been a tremendous increase in efforts to stem the tide of smoking. These efforts have focused both on treatment of the nicotine dependent smoker and on prevention of this destructive behavior. As a result of these endeavors, the overall prevalence rates have significantly declined (Gilpin, Lee, Evans, & Pierce, 1994). At the same time, a more recent trend suggests that smoking among adolescents may again be on the rise (Johnston, O'Malley, & Bachman, 1996; Nelson et al., 1995). As such, cigarette smoking among youth has recently been referred to as a "pediatric disease" (Kessler et al., 1997).

Increasing rates of smoking among teenagers are disturbing for several reasons. First, it is now well documented that the vast majority of adult smokers began their smoking careers by the age of 18 (Mosbach & Leventhal, 1988; U.S. Surgeon General, 1994). Given the association between smoking in adolescence and resultant health problems in adulthood, initiation and maintenance of smoking during adolescence represent a genuine public health concern. Second, increasing evidence links smoking with adolescent health problems as well (e.g., Bewley & Bland, 1976; Lam, Chung, Betson, Wong, & Hedley, 1998; Prokhorov, Emmons, Pallonen, & Tsoh, 1996a). Finally, the notion that adolescent smokers are addicted to nicotine and, hence, driven by compulsive drug-seeking behavior represents a serious concern above and beyond that posed by the associated health risks. Indeed, a major conclusion of a recent *Report of the Surgeon General* was that "most adolescents [who smoke] are addicted to nicotine and report that they want to quit but are unable to do so; they experience relapse rates and withdrawal symptoms similar to those reported by adults" (US DHHS, 1994).

The notion that most, if not all, adolescent smokers are nicotine dependent necessarily impacts on prevention, treatment, and policy at multiple levels. Yet, as the vast majority of research on nicotine dependence has utilized adult smokers, few serious attempts have been made to document nicotine dependence among adolescents. Thus, several researchers have argued that we still know very little about the phenomenon of nicotine dependence among adolescent smokers (e.g., McNeill, 1991; Shiffman, 1991). As to how this state of affairs came to be, Prokhorov, Pallonen, Fava, Ding, and Niaura (1996b) speculated, "[t]he lack of interest in the study of nicotine dependence in adolescents might be explained by the prime orientation of adolescent research on the prevention of smoking onset along with skepticism with respect to the ability to develop an appreciable degree of nicotine dependence during the relatively short period of adolescence" (p. 118). Whatever the reasons underlying the relative dearth of research on this topic, the result is that we still do not know the extent to which nicotine dependence actually exerts control over the smoking of adolescents.

My intention is to examine the theoretical and empirical bases from which our current understanding of nicotine dependence among adolescents is derived. Considered from a broader perspective, I will address the fundamental question of whether the construct of nicotine dependence is, in fact, applicable to adolescent smokers. Toward this end, I will begin by reviewing current thinking on the construct of nicotine dependence.

NICOTINE DEPENDENCE:
FUNDAMENTAL CONCEPTS

Over the past two decades, tremendous gains have been made in our knowledge of the pathogenesis of nicotine dependence and withdrawal symptoms, as well as in our ability to treat this disorder (Henningfield, Gopalan, & Shiffman, 1998). Nicotine dependence is governed both by positive (e.g., pleasurable relaxation, performance enhancement) and negative (e.g., withdrawal avoidance) reinforcement processes. A fairly reliable withdrawal syndrome has been delineated, and includes symptoms such as anxiety, irritability, depressed mood, difficulty concentrating, decreased heart rate, and insomnia (Hughes, Higgins, & Hatsukami, 1990). We also have learned a great deal about the relapse process (Brigham, Henningfield, & Stitzer, 1990; Shiffman, Paty, Gnys, Kassel, & Hickcox, 1996a; Shiffman et al., 1996b), and have come to recognize just how difficult it can be for smokers to quit, with upwards of 75-80% failing on any given quit attempt (e.g., Garvey, Bliss, Hitchcock, Heinold, & Rosner, 1992). Moreover, level of nicotine dependence appears to heighten the risk for subsequent relapse among those smokers trying to quit (Killen, Fortmann, Kraemer, Varady, & Newman, 1992).

In fact, there is reason to believe that nicotine may, in some respects, be the most addictive of all drugs; a far greater proportion of those who experiment with smoking appear to progress to dependence relative to users of drugs of abuse like alcohol, marijuana, and even heroin and cocaine. Interestingly, unlike "harder" drugs, the subjective effects of smoking are subtle. Rarely does a smoker describe that smoking provides them with anything approaching the euphoria or high often attributed to other drugs. And yet, as Shiffman

(1995) observes, " . . . the addictive potential of nicotine is all the more impressive for its ability to engender such compulsive use *without* impressive subjective effects!" (p. 15). Correspondingly, Kozlowski et al. (1989) reported that among a sample of inpatient drug abusers, almost all of them expressed that they derive more pleasure from their drug of choice than they do from smoking. However, the majority also noted that it would be equally or more difficult to quit smoking than to abstain from their particular drug of choice.

In sum, few would disagree with the notion that the addiction liability of cigarette smoking is extremely high (though see Robinson & Pritchard, 1992). Pack-a-day smokers, for example, dose themselves approximately 200 times a day–based on 10 puffs per cigarette × 20 cigarettes a day. Thus, smokers typically self-administer the drug nicotine hundreds-of-thousands of times over the course of a smoking career. These numbers are unrivaled among other drugs of abuse. Given these high rates of drug administration, many would argue that the development of physical dependence is inevitable. In fact, the *exposure* model of drug dependence, which is arguably the most pervasive among competing models, asserts that chronic use of an addictive drug is both a necessary and sufficient cause of addiction. Relative to other drugs of abuse, nicotine seems to be consistent with this model in that relatively few regular smokers are able to avoid becoming dependent on nicotine.

However, there are exceptions to this rule that are worth noting. Our research group (e.g., Shiffman, Paty, Kassel, Gnys, & Zettler-Segal, 1994a; Kassel, Shiffman, Gnys, Paty, & Zettler-Segal, 1994) has described an anomalous group of smokers (*chippers*) who have smoked regularly, and done so for years, without having become dependent on nicotine (see also Gilpin, Cavin, & Pierce, 1997; Owen, Kent, Wakefield, & Roberts, 1995). Though chippers smoke very little (from 1-5 cigarettes a day, at least four days a week), they plainly defy our understanding of drug abuse as put forth by the exposure model of dependence. Interestingly, chippers also appear to resemble, in many respects, the novice, adolescent smoker; they smoke relatively infrequently and their smoking appears to be governed more by psychosocial than by pharmacological or addiction-related motives (Shiffman, Kassel, Paty, Gnys, & Zettler-Segal, 1994b). Thus, one hypothesis is that chippers, for whatever reasons, became "fixated" at an early stage of smoking development and, hence, failed to progress to dependence. Inherent in such a conceptualization is that most adolescents progress through a developmental sequence of smoking behavior that inevitably results in nicotine addiction. However, there exists the possibility that some adolescent smokers remain non-dependent smokers or, after periods of experimentation, simply quit smoking. These important issues will be addressed in more detail shortly.

Measurement Issues

Nicotine dependence is usually assessed by some form of self-report, with the Fagerstrom Tolerance Questionnaire (FTQ; Fagerstrom, 1978) or one of its derivatives (Heatherton, Kozlowski, Frecker, & Fagerstrom, 1991; Tate & Schmitz, 1993) serving as the most widely used measures. Based on clinical observation and a rational-intuitive approach, the FTQ is a short questionnaire that queries smokers on items such as how soon they smoke after waking up in the morning, how many cigarettes they smoke a day, how deeply they inhale, and whether they smoke when they are so ill that they are bed-ridden. Although support for the validity of the FTQ has been reported (Fagerstrom & Schneider, 1989), others have questioned its psychometric properties (Lichtenstein & Mermelstein, 1986) and its ability to assess physical dependence (Lombardo, Hughes, & Fross, 1988).

Some argue the FTQ embodies a rather limited concept of dependence (Shiffman, Hickcox, Gnys, Paty, & Kassel, 1995a), and suggest a broader range of measures should be used to assess nicotine dependence. The *Diagnostic and Statistical Manual of Mental Disorders*–Version IV (American Psychiatric Association, 1994) diagnostic criteria for nicotine dependence are one example of such a broader measure. The DSM-IV conceptualization of substance dependence was greatly influenced by the earlier work of Edwards (Edwards & Gross, 1976; Edwards, 1986), who proposed that an alcohol dependence syndrome could be defined as a narrowing of the drinking repertoire, drink-seeking behavior, tolerance, withdrawal, drinking to relieve or avoid withdrawal symptoms, subjective awareness of the compulsion to drink, and a return to drinking after a period of abstinence. Although this definition of the dependence construct was initially limited to alcohol, many believe that it adequately captures the phenomenon of dependence across most drugs of abuse. DSM-IV's criteria for substance dependence include the presence of at least three of the following: tolerance, withdrawal, use of the substance in larger amounts or over a longer period of time than intended, unsuccessful attempts or a desire to cut down or quit, a great deal of time spent consuming the drug, activities given up or reduced in order to use the drug, and continued use despite knowledge of negative consequences. Interestingly, DSM-IV also permits the subtyping of dependence based on the presence or absence of tolerance and withdrawal.[1]

Several biological indices have also been used as a means of inferring level of nicotine dependence. Cotinine, a metabolite of nicotine, has been used as an indirect measure of nicotine dependence in several studies, yielding mixed findings (e.g., Dozois, Farrow, & Miser, 1995; McNeill, Jarvis, Stapleton, West, & Bryant, 1989; Rojas, Killen, Haydel, Robinson, 1998). Expired air carbon monoxide level, as well as thiocyanate (a derivative of cyanogens found in tobacco smoke), have also been used with some success in determining level of smoking addiction (Noland et al., 1988; Pechacek et al., 1984).

In sum, a variety of measures have been developed as a means of assessing nicotine dependence. It is probably fair to say that operationalization of the construct of nicotine dependence is still a work in progress, and as such, there is no gold standard with respect to its assessment.[2]

NICOTINE DEPENDENCE AMONG ADOLESCENT SMOKERS

What Proportion of Adolescent Smokers are Addicted?

Despite the inherent importance of the subject, relatively few attempts have been made to actually assess nicotine dependence among adolescents. Moreover, a review of this research must be prefaced by the observation that differences both among sample characteristics and in the operationalization of the construct of nicotine dependence render interpretation of these studies difficult. These issues notwithstanding, the findings of several recent studies have provided some insight into the prevalence of nicotine dependence in the adolescent population (see Table 1). For example, Stanton (1995), using DSM-III-R (American Psychiatric Association, 1987) criteria, assessed nicotine dependence in a sample of 18-year-olds who smoked daily for at least one month. Results indicated that 56.4% of these adolescents met criteria for nicotine dependence. Gritz et al. (1998) sampled 76 5th-12th graders who were classified as "current smokers" (smoked at least one cigarette a month) and used a modified version of the FTQ. Here, 35.5% of the sample was classified as "moderately" dependent, whereas 7.9% were "substantially" dependent on nicotine. Dozois et al. (1995) interviewed 57 incarcerated adolescents, ages 12-17, using the Fagerstrom Test for Nicotine Dependence (Heatherton et al., 1986), and reported that 42.3% met criteria for nicotine dependence. In this study, no specific criteria were listed as to what constitutes classification as a smoker. Finally, Prokhorov et al. (1996b) assessed dependence in vocational-technical school 10th-12th grade students who had volunteered to participate in a smoking cessation program. Based on a modified FTQ, almost 20% of these students appeared to meet criteria for "substantial" nicotine dependence.

Taken together, the results of these studies suggest that between 8% and 56% of adolescent smokers are addicted to nicotine. As noted earlier, however, there are marked differences in the sample characteristics that likely contribute to the inconsistent findings. For example, the Stanton (1995) study, which reported the highest prevalence of dependence, sampled adolescents who were daily smokers, whereas the Gritz et al. (1998) investigation assessed students who smoked at least one cigarette a month. Furthermore, the methods by which nicotine dependence was assessed differed markedly.

TABLE 1. Recent Studies Examining Nicotine Dependence Among Adolescent Smokers

Study	Sample Characteristics	Age/Grade	N	Assessment of Nicotine Dependence (ND)	Assessed Withdrawal Symptoms (WS)	Biological Index	% Meeting Criteria for Nicotine Dependence
Stanton, 1995	New Zealand birth cohort; daily smokers for ≥1 month	18	321	DSM-III-R criteria[a]	Yes; 75% report experiencing WS	Cotinine (unrelated to ND)	56.4
Fergusson, Lynskey, & Horwood, 1996	New Zealand birth cohort; reported smokers (no specific criteria given)	16	947	DSM-III-R criteria[b]	No	None	Not reported
Gritz, Prokhorov et al., 1998	Public school students; "current smokers" who smoke ≥1 cig a month	5th-12th grade	76	Modified 7-item Fagerstrom Tolerance Questionnaire	Yes; data not reported	Saliva cotinine; 70% of smokers correctly classified	35.5 ("Moderate") 7.9 ("Substantial")
Prokhorov, Pallonen et al., 1996	Vocational-technical school students; smokers who volunteered for smoking cessation program	10th-12th grade	110	Modified 7-item Fagerstrom Tolerance Questionnaire	No	None	19.8 ("Substantial")
Rojas, Killen, Haydel, & Robinson, 1998	High school students; smoked ≥1 cig in past 30 days and had ≥1 previous quit attempt	10th grade	249	Modified 5-item Fagerstrom Tolerance Questionnaire	Yes; WS significantly correlated with ND	Saliva cotinine; correlates .31 with ND	Not reported
Dozois, Farrow, & Miser, 1995	Incarcerated adolescent smokers (no specific criteria given)	12-17	57	Fagerstrom Test for Nicotine Dependence	Yes; craving most prominent	Urinary Cotinine; poor predictor of WS	42.3

Notes. [a] assessed via Diagnostic Interview Schedule (3 Section A criteria and 1 Section B criteria).
[b] assessed via self-report (5 cigs a day and 2 symptoms of ND)

Moreover, some studies using the same diagnostic tool have employed the tool differently (e.g., compare Stanton, 1995, and Fergusson, Lynskey, & Horwood, 1996 in Table 1). Despite these methodological difficulties, it appears that a significant proportion of adolescent smokers (however defined) are dependent on nicotine (however defined); conversely, it appears that a significant proportion of adolescent smokers are *not* nicotine dependent. It should be acknowledged, however, that just because they are not dependent at one point in time does not preclude the possibility of adolescents becoming dependent at some future point in time (see next section on Developmental Trajectory).

Withdrawal Symptoms. Given that tolerance and withdrawal are among the cardinal symptoms of drug dependence, an examination of withdrawal symptoms could help clarify the nature of nicotine dependence in adolescents. The most in-depth study of this particular issue was conducted by McNeill and colleagues (McNeill, West, Jarvis, Jackson, & Bryant, 1986). One hundred and sixteen female adolescent smokers were asked about withdrawal symptoms they experienced during past quit attempts. Sixty-three percent reported experiencing some withdrawal, with "a strong need to smoke" and "hungry" the two most commonly experienced effects. Interestingly, even among occasional (non-daily) smokers, 47% described experiencing some level of withdrawal distress. Reported experience of withdrawal symptoms was positively related to self-reports of cigarette consumption, depth of inhalation, and salivary cotinine concentrations. The results of this study suggest that adolescent smokers are likely to suffer withdrawal symptoms when they try to quit smoking, thus implicating pharmacological factors even in this relatively early stage of smoking.

Similar findings regarding withdrawal symptoms among adolescents have been reported by others (see Table 1). In one study of 249 high-school smokers, 30.5% reported no withdrawal symptoms during previous attempts to quit smoking, while 35% reported more than two symptoms (Rojas et al., 1998). "Craving" (45.4%) and "nervous and tense" (31.8%) were the most widely endorsed symptoms. A total withdrawal index was also calculated and found to correlate significantly ($r = .51, p < .001$) with a measure of nicotine dependence (modified FTQ), but only moderately with saliva cotinine ($r = .15, p = .03$). Stanton (1995) found that 75% of 18-year-old smokers reported having experienced withdrawal symptoms, with craving again emerging as the most prevalent symptom (61%), followed by irritability or anger (43%). Dozois et al. (1995) described that, among incarcerated adolescent smokers, "cravings" (80%) and increased "irritability, frustration, and temper" (68%) were the most commonly experienced withdrawal symptoms.

In sum, it appears that the majority of adolescent smokers report withdrawal symptoms during quit attempts.[3] At the same time, it is important to remember that most of the criteria comprising withdrawal are subjective in nature, and as such, are prone to expectancy biases and misattributions. Interestingly, across the four described studies, craving, or desire to smoke, consistently emerged as the most commonly reported withdrawal symptom, even though it is not considered a component of tobacco dependence in DSM-IV (American Psychiatric Association, 1994). The exclusion of craving from diagnostic consideration likely arises from the controversy surrounding its measurement and validity as a psychological construct (see Hughes et al., 1990; Kassel & Shiffman, 1992).

Subjective Effects. Subjective effects experienced by smokers likely reflect the role of nicotine (and other constituents of tobacco smoke) in governing smoking behavior. Thus, assessment of subjective effects in adolescent smokers may help to clarify how rapidly pharmacological motives take on significance. McNeill, Jarvis, and West (1987) found that 82% of a sample of 170 female adolescent smokers reported experiencing at least one of five specified subjective effects of smoking. Feeling calmer was the most frequently endorsed effect and daily smokers were more likely to report this than non-daily smokers (64% versus 38%, respectively). Moreover, the likelihood of experiencing at least one withdrawal symptom when trying to quit was greater among those who reported feeling calmer when smoking (84% versus 40%). Other subjective effects of smoking received relatively little endorsement, with 34% experiencing dizziness and lightheadedness, 15% describing feeling sick, 8% experiencing greater alertness, and 1% feeling "high." The salience of relaxation motives for smoking among adolescents is supported by Dozois et al. (1995), who found that 80% of adolescent smokers smoke "to help relax." Taken together, these results indicate that subjective effects of smoking are commonly reported by adolescents, which again implicates pharmacological factors (in addition to psychosocial factors) early on in the development of smoking behavior.

Desire to Quit Smoking. Popular conceptualizations of addictive behavior emphasize the desire on the part of substance-dependent individuals to cease the behavior. In fact, unsuccessful attempts or a desire to cut down or quit is one of the criteria for substance dependence according to DSM-IV (American Psychiatric Association, 1994). Several investigators have queried adolescent smokers regarding their desire to quit. Sargent, Mott, and Stevens (1998) reported that 26% of their sample of high-school smokers expressed a desire to quit, while 27% reported at least one unsuccessful quit attempt. Interestingly, most students with strong intentions to quit smoking were "occasional" smokers, 61% of whom actually succeeded, compared with only 19% of all other smokers combined, and only 6.8% of daily smokers. The authors interpret these data as consistent with elements of both the addiction and stage models (to be discussed shortly) of smoking behavior.

McNeill et al. (1986) found that most teenage smokers perceived themselves to be dependent on cigarettes and that, even within their first year of smoking, reported wanting to stop, having tried to, and suffering withdrawal symptoms when doing so. Pallonen, Prochaska, Velicer, Prokhorov, and Smith (1998) similarly reported that about half of the current high-school smokers in their study reported a desire to quit. In a sample of tenth grade smokers, Rojas et al. (1998) found 51% reported a previous attempt to quit smoking for good. As noted earlier, a significant proportion (35%) of these students also experienced more than two withdrawal symptoms during these quit attempts. Interestingly, one study reported no significant differences in the percentages of those who were or were not classified as dependent and whether or not they had tried to quit or cut down on smoking in the past (Stanton, 1995). Stanton's findings suggest that unsuccessful quit attempts may not be a direct reflection of nicotine dependence.

In sum, it appears that many adolescents who smoke regularly want to quit. Indeed, between 55 and 65% of smokers ages 12 to 18 years report having tried to stop. The extent to which both desire to quit smoking and failed quit attempts are directly attributable to nicotine dependence is still not known, but certainly deserves continued empirical evaluation.

Biological Indices of Dependence

As nicotine dependence is believed to be based on an internally driven motive to smoke, it is conceivable that biological indices of smoking (e.g., cotinine, expired air carbon monoxide) might serve as reasonable markers of dependence among adolescent smokers. Whereas ample evidence points to the ability of cotinine, thiocyanate, and carbon monoxide to discriminate nonsmokers and smokers (e.g., Noland et al., 1988; Gritz et al., 1998), the validity of these measures as proxies for nicotine dependence is less clear. For example, Stanton (1995) reported that although cotinine levels in saliva were positively related to level of cigarette consumption, they were not meaningfully correlated with a measure of nicotine dependence. Dozois et al. (1995) examined the association between urinary cotinine and withdrawal symptoms, observing little correspondence between the two during a period of enforced tobacco abstinence. Rojas et al. (1998) reported significant, yet moderate, correlations between saliva cotinine levels and nicotine dependence ($r = .31$), withdrawal symptoms ($r = .15$), and cigarettes smoked during last 30 days ($r = .44$).

To date, the utility of biochemical measures as markers of nicotine dependence is still questionable. It may be that biochemical tests cannot typically detect the low levels of smoking characteristic of this age level (Klesges, Klesges, & Cigrang, 1992). At the same time, McNeill et al. (1986) reported significant correlations between salivary cotinine and weekly consumption (r = .59), self-reported depth of inhalation (r = .48), and overall withdrawal scores (r = .43) in a sample of adolescent schoolgirls. Moreover, McNeill et al. (1989) found that cotinine levels increased substantially over time, with the greatest rise occurring during the transition from occasional to daily smoking. Cotinine concentrations at the beginning of this longitudinal study were substantial, with approximately half of the average adult concentration observed in these 11- to 14-year-old daily smokers. When followed two years later, the same group of smokers evidenced levels more than two-thirds of the average adult concentration. In sum, though biochemical indices of smoking behavior have yielded mixed findings across numerous studies, their use is warranted in that they add to a more comprehensive assessment of smoking behavior and appear particularly helpful in the context of longitudinal tracking of smoking behavior.

Developmental Trajectory

As noted earlier, some have insinuated that nicotine dependence is of little relevance to adolescent smokers as adolescence provides too narrow a window of opportunity within which to develop dependence. Implicit in such a view is the notion that progression to addiction take a long time. But how much time? What is the developmental trajectory of nicotine dependence?

Stage Models. In an effort to delineate the processes governing smoking progression, several developmental-stage models have been put forth. Russell (1971) proposed a model wherein the development of dependence proceeds through three primary stages. During the first stage, smokers smoke for psychosocial motives, prompted by friends and social situations in which smoking is normative. Consistent with Russell's notion, a wealth of data has since emerged implicating the role of social modeling in early smoking (e.g., Botvin et al., 1993; Chassin, Presson, Sherman, Corty, & Olshavsky, 1984; Ferguson et al., 1992; Wang, Fitzhugh, Eddy, Fu, & Turner, 1997). Most smokers are then believed to progress rapidly to the second stage, in which their smoking is driven by the pharmacological effects of nicotine via positive reinforcement. At this stage, smokers seek both the relaxing and stimulating effects of the drug. Thus, this model implies that the pharmacologically reinforcing effects of nicotine only accidentally come into play during the progression toward regular smoking.[4] Some smokers then progress to a third stage where their smoking is primarily governed by the need to stave off or escape from withdrawal symptoms (negative reinforcement). It is believed that the vast majority of adult, dependent smokers are stage three smokers. Factor analysis of a self-report smoking motives questionnaire administered to a wide range of smokers supported the basic tenets of this model (Russell, Peto, & Patel, 1974).

Hirschman, Leventhal, and Glynn (1984) interviewed schoolchildren in grades 3 through 10 about their smoking experiences and described a stage-model that emphasized early experience with smoking. Four specific stages were defined as: tried tobacco, progressed to second cigarette, progressed to third cigarette, and progressed to current smoking. Of the 47% of the sample who had ever tried a cigarette, only 32% reported trying a second, while 77% of the second-triers went on to smoke a third cigarette. Of those who smoked a third, 57% reported current smoking. Of note, various factors played differential roles across each stage. For example, propensity toward risk-taking differentiated those who ever-tried from those who did not. Those adolescents who quickly progressed to a second cigarette were characterized by life stress variables, while those who smoked a third cigarette could be characterized by having had a very brief delay between their first two cigarettes.

Hirschman et al. (1984) also found that reaction to the first cigarette was a key variable in predicting subsequent behavior: Those who experienced coughing (a peripheral effect) were less likely to smoke a second cigarette, while those who reported dizziness (a central effect) progressed relatively quickly to a second cigarette (see also Flay, Davernas, Best, Kersell, & Ryan, 1983).

Interestingly, these findings parallel those reported by Shiffman (1989) in his study of chippers (non-dependent smokers). Although it was hypothesized that chippers' lack of progress toward addictive smoking might have resulted from an unusually aversive response to their first cigarette, the opposite finding emerged: Chippers reported significantly fewer severe side effects as a consequence of their first cigarette relative to those individuals who went on to become "regular" smokers. Moreover, in spite of their relatively benign initial response, chippers progressed far more slowly to their second cigarette, as well as to monthly, weekly, and daily smoking. Taken together, these findings are consistent with a sensitivity model of dependence, in which heightened sensitivity to nicotine is thought to play an even more important role than the traditionally emphasized tolerance in the development of dependence (Pomerleau, Collins, Shiffman, & Pomerleau, 1993).

Finally, another influential stage model (Flay, 1993) posits that smokers progress through the following five discreet stages: (a) the preparatory stage, in which attitudes toward nicotine and its perceived functions are formed, (b) the initial trying stage, which includes smoking the first two to three cigarettes, usually in a social context, and the resulting physiological and psychosocial reinforcements obtained, (c) the experimentation stage, which includes situational-specific irregular use over an extended period of time, (d) regular use, during which the adolescent smokes on a regular basis (e.g., weekends or daily), and (e) nicotine dependence or addiction, in which smoking is governed predominantly by an internally regulated need for nicotine. Data that identify predictors of transitions through these stages are just beginning to appear (Flay, Hu, & Richardson, 1998) and should begin to shed light on the processes governing development of nicotine dependence.

Implicit in most of the stage models is the idea that although early smoking experience is socially reinforced, progression through the stages leads to an internally driven drive state. However, few studies have assessed the reported changes in smoking motives over time, motives that should, according to these models, reflect these developmental changes. McGee and Stanton (1993) examined whether reasons for smoking at age 13 were associated with smoking rate at age 15. Their questionnaire assessed three groups of smoking motives: relaxation, friends (social), and image, none of which predicted smoking in later adolescence. Surprisingly, these researchers did not assess an "addiction" motive, nor did they report whether smoking motives actually changed over the two-year period. A recent cross-sectional study found smoking to relax (80%), to help cope with boredom (46%) and because of nicotine addiction (46%) were the three motives most often cited by incarcerated adolescent smokers (Dozois et al., 1995). Assessment of smoking motives among adolescents is crucial in order to more fully understand the motivational processes governing smoking behavior across various developmental stages. Clearly, longitudinal studies are needed that track the developmental progress of adolescent smokers in order to determine whether stage-modeling is a valid phenomenon, as well as to assess which smokers are most susceptible to subsequent nicotine dependence.

Put simply, although developmental stage models of nicotine dependence hold intuitive appeal, they still remain the subject of relatively little research. The majority of studies of smoking initiation have simply compared smokers, regardless of their level of use, to nonsmokers. Moreover, even fewer attempts have been made to delineate factors that might differentiate initial use from continued use, or from eventual nicotine dependence. Potential moderators of stage-specific risk factors (e.g., sex, race/ethnicity, depression, body weight concerns) are beginning to receive attention, though the findings are thus far inconsistent (e.g., Ary & Biglan, 1988; Chassin, Presson, Sherman, Montello, & McGrew, 1986; Gritz et al., 1998; Robinson, Klesges, Zbikowski, & Glaser, 1997). Finally, the results from one well-designed longitudinal study yielded findings at odds with stage-modeling. McNeill and colleagues (McNeill et al., 1986, 1987, 1989) found that even within their first year of smoking, a majority of adolescent schoolgirls reported perceiving themselves as dependent on cigarettes, wanting to stop smoking, having tried to quit, and suffering aversive withdrawal symptoms when doing so. Thus, these girls appear to have either moved quite rapidly through the various developmental smoking stages or to have skipped over the earlier stages altogether, as their smoking was reportedly governed by pharmacological factors shortly after initiation.

Which Smokers Progress to Nicotine Dependence? As discussed earlier, the few cross-sectional studies that have been conducted suggest that relatively small, yet significant, proportions of adolescent smokers are likely nicotine dependent. Though stage-models propose a series of processes through which some, but not all, smokers proceed, they do not fully address what is perhaps the most critical question with respect to developmental trajectory: What proportion of those who experiment with smoking will progress to nicotine dependence? The results from several longitudinal investigations are beginning begin to shed light on this question. Russell (1990), drawing upon data from an earlier British survey of 984 adults (McKennell & Thomas, 1967), asserted that of those who smoke as little as one cigarette, 70% go on to smoke regularly for five years or more; of those who smoke more than one cigarette, 82% become regular smokers; and those who smoke four or more cigarettes have a 94% chance of becoming long-term regular smokers. These data are particularly compelling and suggest that even brief adolescent experimentation with smoking inevitably leads to a career of regular smoking that typically lasts from 30-40 years (Russell, 1990).

Other investigations, however, have yielded more conservative findings. Hirschman et al. (1984) suggest that only one third to one half of adolescents who experiment with cigarettes go on to become regular smokers. Similarly, McNeill (1991) reports that in a longitudinal study of 11 to 13 year-old British schoolchildren, 55% of triers (smoked one or two cigarettes) went on to further experimentation over the next 2 1/2 years. Of these 55%, 33% had "taken up smoking" and 22% described that they "used to smoke." So while some (33%) progressed to regular smoking, 22% actually quit smoking during this time period. Flint, Yamada, and Novotny (1998) describe that among white teenagers who were smoking "experimenters" at baseline, only 26% progressed to current smoking assessed four years later. For black teens, the percentage who progressed to current smoking was even lower (10%). An important implication of these various studies is that early experimentation does not appear to inevitably lead to regular use or nicotine dependence. In fact, the majority of experimenters did not become addicted smokers.

Choi, Pierce, Gilpin, Farkas, and Berry (1997) recently examined the progression from smoking experimentation (had at least a puff but had not smoked > 100 cigarettes) to established smoking (smoked > 100 cigarettes in lifetime). A nationally representative sample of adolescents between 12 and 18 was screened at baseline and then four years later. Similar to McNeill's (1991) findings, results indicated that 31% of the baseline experimenters had progressed to established smoking. Keep in mind that "established smoking" is not synonymous with dependence. Therefore, it is likely that even fewer than 31% of these would actually meet criteria for nicotine dependence. Again, these data are consistent with the notion that although experimentation may be a necessary step toward becoming an addicted smoker, many adolescents who have experimented with cigarettes do not progress to meet the adult definition of either a current smoker (smoked 100 cigarettes in lifetime and currently smokes) or an addicted smoker (Flay et al., 1983; U.S. Surgeon General, 1994).

Finally, Pierce and Gilpin (1996) estimated the expected smoking duration for white, adolescent smokers who had started smoking recently. Based on a median initiation age of 16 to 17 years, their model predicts that 50% of adolescent males will smoke for at least another 16 years, while 50% of adolescent females will smoke for at least 20 years. Put another way, the median cessation age for those who start smoking as adolescents is expected to be 33 for males and 37 for females. These data suggest that a significant proportion of adolescent smokers will likely progress to dependence during their smoking careers. Correspondingly, results from another longitudinal study (Chassin, Presson, Sherman, & Edwards, 1990) indicate that relative to adolescent nonsmokers, adolescent smokers were 16 times more likely to make the transition to young adult smoker. Moreover, even infrequent experimentation in adolescence was associated with significantly increased risk for young adult smoking. Thus, from the perspective of relative risk, any smoking in adolescence greatly heightens risk for subsequent smoking in adulthood.

DISCUSSION

Becoming a smoker, particularly an addicted smoker, is a complex developmental process. A host of factors (e.g., psychosocial, physiological, cultural, genetic) likely play differential and important roles in determining smoking behavior, from acquisition through cessation. In fact, the emergence of models that combine acquisition and cessation stages appear promising in that they provide a more comprehensive understanding of adolescent cigarette smoking (Flay, Ockene, & Tager, 1992; Pallonen et al., 1998).

One of the questions posed at the outset of this article was: Is the construct of nicotine dependence suitable and appropriate for use with adolescent smokers? My answer is a qualified "yes." Adolescent smoking initiation is a growing and serious health problem. It has been shown that a significant proportion of adolescents will progress to lengthy smoking careers as dependent smokers and, hence, place themselves at heightened risk for the associated health consequences. It follows that adequate operationalization and assessment of nicotine dependence among adolescents should be of primary concern to health professionals across all levels of inquiry–from basic science to clinical work to public policy. Given the importance of this problem, it is disconcerting that a review of the literature reveals a relative dearth of research on the topic of nicotine dependence among adolescents. The majority of studies on adolescent smoking have assessed indices such as frequency of smoking and number of cigarettes smoked, assigned arbitrary labels (e.g., "current," "light," or "regular" smoker), and in many instances *inferred* the presence of nicotine dependence. What we do not yet know, however, is whether the development of dependence actually parallels increases in smoking rate and frequency. Among adult smokers, smoking rate is at best an imperfect marker of dependence. Among adolescents, the association between smoking rate and dependence likely may be even more inconsistent.

It has also been shown that a significant proportion of adolescents who smoke do not progress to nicotine dependence. Thus, treating (in both the vernacular and clinical sense) all adolescent smokers as a homogenous group represents a grievous error. Delineation of both predisposing and protective factors is critical in bettering our understanding of the dependence process. Careful study of the development of dependence could also shed light on other pertinent issues. The following questions posed by Shiffman (1991) still remain unanswered: "Does addiction develop gradually, or is the process marked by abrupt changes? What is the role of external influences, such as restrictive smoking policies and their developmental trajectory (e.g., less restriction in smoking on exit from school) in the escalation of smoking? Are there key markers of the transition to dependent smoking–e.g., solitary smoking (indicating independence from immediate social influences), morning smoking (see Kozlowski, Director, & Harford, 1981), or negative affect smoking (Ashton & Stepney, 1982)?" (pgs. 613-614). These are all critical questions, the answers to which should help clarify the nature of adolescent smoking dependence.

In sum, a review of the literature on adolescent smoking behavior reveals marked variation both within and across adolescent smokers. Some appear able to dabble with smoking and then cease the behavior. Others progress on to more regular smoking, yet still remain non-dependent smokers. Still others ultimately become hooked, a process which can occur quite quickly (McNeill, 1986, 1987) or more slowly. Acknowledging variability in smoking behavior is at odds with the exposure, or addiction, model of dependence described earlier in this article. As articulated by Shiffman (1991), it may be time for a re-evaluation and refinement of our current models of dependence. Future models will need to take into account three potential sources of variation in smoking behavior and nicotine addiction: (1) variability among individuals, (2) variability within individuals across time and situations, and (3) variability in developmental progression of smoking, which serves as a specific source of within-person variability (Shiffman, 1991).

With respect to adolescent smoking, it is this last source of variation that is most pertinent and in need of incorporation into models of nicotine dependence. Though acknowledgment of the fact that not all adolescents who smoke are dependent or will become so may be at odds with some pervasive models of addiction, its acceptance will allow for a more thorough and complete investigation into the processes governing the development of nicotine dependence.

Treatment and intervention programs for the adolescent smoker would also benefit from an individual-differences approach that acknowledges variation in the development of smoking. Hence, treatments may need to be tailored to the specific characteristics of the adolescent smoker. For example, the extent to which nicotine replacement therapy is warranted may be a function of level of dependence, number of cigarettes smoked a day, motives for smoking, and other factors (see Patten, this publication). An even more radical consideration is whether, from a public health perspective, low-level (non-dependent) smoking is an acceptable outcome for some adolescent smokers (Hughes, 1998). Indeed, harm-reduction approaches have been receiving more attention in the past few years and are emerging as a possible treatment alternative for some smokers (Hughes, 1995).

In conclusion, no one would argue that adolescent smoking is an acceptable behavior. Yet, we cannot ignore the fact that more adolescents have been taking up smoking in recent years. Increased efforts should be employed to better understand the developmental processes underlying nicotine dependence. Through the development and utilization of precise measures and adequate sampling strategies, we will begin to understand the key factors influencing adolescent smoking, and ultimately develop more effective prevention and treatment strategies.

NOTES

1. The only self-report questionnaire of which I am aware that is based on Edward's concept of a dependence syndrome and used to assess nicotine dependence is the Nicotine Dependence Syndrome Scale, which appears to capture aspects of nicotine dependence not tapped by the FTQ (Shiffman et al., 1995a).

2. The potential confusion resulting from differential operationalization of the construct of nicotine dependence is demonstrated by the findings of a recent study (Kawakami, Takatsuka, Shimizu, & Takai, 1998) that assessed nicotine dependence in Japanese male ever-smokers using the following criteria: International Classification of Disease (ICD-10), DSM-III-R, DSM-IV, and the FTQ. Resultant life-time prevalence rates of nicotine dependence were 42%, 26%, 32%, and 19% according to ICD-10, DSM-III-R, DSM-IV, and FTQ, respectively.

3. By comparison, chippers (non-dependent smokers) who underwent two days of abstinence did not manifest any symptoms of withdrawal as assessed in a naturalistic

field study (Shiffman, Paty, Gnys, Elash, & Kassel, 1995b). Moreover, rather than just relying on subjective accounts of "difficulty concentrating," this study employed computerized technology through which valid cognitive performance assessments were made.

4. As Shiffman (1991) noted, the alleged pharmacologically reinforcing effects of nicotine, such as mood management and performance enhancement, are hardly robust and reliable phenomena. The extent to which they exist among adult smokers is still open to much discussion and debate (see, e.g., Heishman, Taylor, & Henningfield, 1994; Kassel, 1997; Parrott, 1994; West, 1993). Thus, it has yet to be adequately demonstrated that such effects play an important role in governing the smoking of adolescents.

REFERENCES

American Psychiatric Association. (1987). *Diagnostic and statistical manual of mental disorders, third edition, revised.* Washington, DC: American Psychiatric Association.

American Psychiatric Association. (1994). *Diagnostic and statistical manual of mental disorders, fourth edition.* Washington, DC: American Psychiatric Association.

Ary, D. V., & Biglan, A. (1988). Longitudinal changes in adolescent cigarette smoking behavior: Onset and cessation. *Journal of Behavioral Medicine, 11,* 361-381.

Ashton, H., & Stepney, R. (1982). *Smoking: Psychology and pharmacology.* London: Tavistock Press.

Bewley, B. R., & Bland, J. M. (1976). Smoking and respiratory symptoms in two groups of school children. *Preventive Medicine, 5,* 63-69.

Botvin, G. J., Baker, E., Botvin, E. M., Dusenbury, L., Cardwell, J., & Diaz, T. (1993). Factors promoting cigarette smoking among black youth: A causal modeling approach. *Addictive Behaviors, 18,* 397-405.

Brigham, J., Henningfield, J. E., & Stitzer, M. L. (1990). Smoking relapse: A review. *International Journal of the Addictions, 25,* 12239-1255.

Chassin, L., Presson, C. C., Sherman, S. J., Corty, E., & Olshavsky, R. (1984). Predicting the onset of cigarette smoking in adolescents: A longitudinal study. *Journal of Applied Social Psychology, 14,* 224-243.

Chassin, L., Presson, C. C., Sherman, S. J., & Edwards, D. A. (1990). The natural history of cigarette smoking: Predicting young adult smoking outcomes from adolescent smoking patterns. *Health Psychology, 9,* 701-716.

Chassin, L., Presson, C. C., Sherman, S. J., Montello, D., & McGrew, J. (1986). Changes in peer and parent influence during adolescence: Longitudinal versus cross-sectional perspectives on smoking initiation. *Developmental Psychology, 22,* 327-334.

Choi, W. S., Pierce, J. P., Gilpin, E. A., Farkas, A. J., & Berry, C. C. (1997). Which adolescent experimenters progress to established smoking in the United States. *American Journal of Preventive Medicine, 13,* 385-391.

Dozois, D. N., Farrow, J. A., & Miser, A. (1995). Smoking patterns and cessation motivations during adolescence. *The International Journal of the Addictions, 30,* 1485-1498.

Edwards, G. (1986). The alcohol dependence syndrome: A concept as stimulus to enquiry. *British Journal of Addiction, 81,* 171-183.

Edwards, G., & Gross, M. M. (1976). Alcohol dependence: Provisional description of a clinical syndrome. *British Medical Journal, 1,* 1058-1061.

Fagerstrom, K. O. (1978). Measuring degree of physical dependence to tobacco smoking with reference to individualization of treatment. *Addictive Behaviors, 3,* 235-241.

Fagerstrom, K. O., & Schneider, N. (1989). Measuring nicotine dependence: A review of the Fagerstrom Tolerance Questionnaire. *Journal of Behavioral Medicine, 12,* 159-182.

Ferguson, K. J., Burke, J. A., Becker, S. L., Reimers, T. M., Daughety, V. S., & Pomrehn, P. R. (1992). The recruitment of new smokers by adolescents. *Health Communication, 4,* 171-181.

Fergusson, D. M., Lynskey, M. T., & Horwood, J. (1996). Comorbidity between depressive disorders and nicotine dependence in a cohort of 16-year-olds. *Archives of General Psychiatry, 53.*

Flay, B. R. (1993). Youth tobacco use: Risks, patterns, and control. In J. Slade & C. T. Orleans (Eds.), *Nicotine addiction: Principles and management* (pp. 365-384). New York: Oxford University Press.

Flay, B. R., dAvernas, J. R., Best, J. A., Kersell, M. W., & Ryan, K. B. (1983). Cigarette smoking: Why young people do it and ways of preventing it. In P. J. McGrath & P. Firestone (Eds.), *Pediatric and adolescent behavioral medicine: Issues in treatment.* (Vol. 10,). New York: Springer.

Flay, B. R., Hu, F. B., & Richardson, J. (1998). Psychosocial predictors of different stages of cigarette smoking among high school students. *Preventive Medicine, 27,* A9-A18.

Flay, B. R., Ockene, J. K., & Tager, I. B. (1992). Smoking: Epidemiology, cessation, and prevention. *Chest, 102, 277S-301S.*

Flint, A. J., Yamada, E. G., & Novotny, T. E. (1998). Black-white differences in cigarette smoking uptake: Progression from adolescent experimentation to regular use. *Preventive Medicine, 27,* 358-364.

Garvey, A. J., Bliss, R. E., Hitchcock, J. L., Heinold, J. W., & Rosner, B. (1992). Predictors of smoking relapse among self-quitters: A report from the normative aging study. *Addictive Behaviors, 17,* 367-377.

Gilpin, E., Cavin, S. W., & Pierce, J. P. (1997). Adult smokers who do not smoke daily. *Addiction, 92,* 473-480.

Gilpin, E. A., Lee, L., Evans, N., & Pierce, J. P. (1994). Smoking initiation rates in adults and minors: United States 1944-1988. *American Journal of Epidemiology, 140,* 535-543.

Gritz, E. R., Prokhorov, A. V., Hudmon, K. S., Chamberlain, R. M., Taylor, W. C., DiClemente, C. C., Johnston, D. A., Hu, S., Jones, L. A., Jones, M. M., Rosenblum, C. K., Ayars, C. L., & Amos, C. I. (1998). Cigarette smoking in a multiethnic population of youth: Methods and baseline findings. *Preventive Medicine, 27,* 365-384.

Heatherton, T. F., Kozlowski, L. T., Frecker, R. C., & Fagerstrom, K. O. (1991). The Fagerstrom test for nicotine dependence: A revision of the Fagerstrom tolerance questionnaire. *British Journal of Addiction, 86,* 1119-1127.

Heishman, S. J., Taylor, R. C., & Henningfield, J. E. (1994). Nicotine and smoking: A review of effects on human performance. *Experimental and Clinical Psychopharmacology, 2,* 345-395.

Henningfield, J. E., Gopalan, L., & Shiffman, S. (1998). Tobacco dependence: fundamental concepts and recent advances. *Current Opinion in Psychiatry, 11*, 259-263.

Hirschman, R. S., Leventhal, H., & Glynn, K. (1984). The development of smoking behavior: Conceptualization and supportive cross-sectional survey data. *Journal of Applied Social Psychology, 14*, 184-206.

Hughes, J. R. (1995). Applying harm reduction to smoking. *Tobacco Control, 4*, S33-S38.

Hughes, J. R. (1998). Harm-reduction approaches to smoking: The need for data. *America Journal of Preventive Medicine, 15*, 78-79.

Hughes, J. R., Higgins, S. T., & Hatsukami, D. (1990). Effects of abstinence from tobacco: A critical review. In L. T. Kozlowski, H. M. Annis, H. D. Cappell, F. B. Glaser, M. S. Goodstat, Y. Israel, H. Kalant, E. M. Seelera, & E. R. Vingilis (Eds.), *Research advances in alcohol and drug problems* (Vol. 10, pp. 317-398). New York: Plenum Publishing.

Johnston, L. D., O'Malley, P. M., & Bachman, J. G. (1996). *National survey results on drug use from the Monitoring the Future Study, 1975-1993. Vols. 1 and 2.* (NIH Publication No. 94-3810). Rockville, MD: United States Department of Health and Human Services.

Kassel, J. D. (1997). Smoking and attention: A review and reformulation of the stimulus-filter hypothesis. *Clinical Psychology review, 17*, 451-478.

Kassel, J. D., & Shiffman, S. (1992). What can hunger teach us about drug craving? A comparative analysis of the two constructs. *Advances in Behaviour Research and Therapy, 14*, 141-167.

Kassel, J. D., Shiffman, S., Gnys, M., Paty, J., & Zettler-Segal, M. (1994). Psychosocial and personality differences in chippers and regular smokers. *Addictive Behaviors, 19*, 565-575.

Kawakami, N., Takatsuka, N., Shimizu, H., & Takai, A. (1998). Life-time prevalence and risk factors of tobacco-nitoine dependence in male ever-smokers in Japan. *Addiction, 93*, 1023-1032.

Kessler, D. A., Natanblut, S. L., Wilkenfeld, J. P., Lorraine, C. C., Mayl, S. L., Bernstein, I. B. G., & Thompson, L. (1997). Nicotine addition: A pediatric disease. *Journal of Pediatrics, 130*, 518-524.

Killen, J. D., Fortmann, S. P., Klaemer, H. C., Varady, A., & Newman, B. (1992). Who will relapse? Symptoms of nicotine dependence predict long-term relapse after smoking cessation. *Journal of Consulting and Clinical Psychology, 60*, 797-801.

Klesges, L. M., Klesges, R. C., & Cigrang, J. A. (1992). Discrepancies between self-reported smoking and carboxyhemoglobin: An analysis of the Second National Health and Nutritional Survey. *American Journal of Public Health, 82*, 1029-1032.

Kozlowski, L. T., Director, J., & Harford, M. A. (1981). Tobacco dependence, restraint and time of the first cigarette of the day. *Addictive Behaviors, 6*, 307-312.

Kozlowski, L. T., Wilkinson, D. A., Skinner, W., Kent, C., Franklin, T., & Pope, M. (1989). Comparing tobacco cigarette dependence with other drug dependencies. Greater or equal 'difficulty quitting' and 'urges to use,' but less 'pleasure' from cigarettes. *Journal of the American Medical Association, 261*, 898-901.

Lam, T. H., Chung, S. F., Betson, C. L., Wong, C. M., & Hedley, A. J. (1998). Respiratory symptoms due to active and passive smoking in junior secondary school students in Hong Kong. *International Journal of Epidemiology, 27*, 41-48.

Lichtenstein, E., & Mermelstein, R. J. (1986). Some methodological cautions in the use of the tolerance questionnaire. *Addictive Behaviors, 11*, 439-442.

Lombardo, T. W., Hughes, J. R., & Fross, J. D. (1988). Failure to support the validity of the Fagerstrom Tolerance questionnaire as a measure of physiological tolerance to nicotine. *Addictive Behaviors, 13*, 87-90.

McGee, R., & Stanton, W. R. (1993). A longitudinal study of reasons for smoking in adolescence. *Addiction, 88*, 265-271.

McGinnis, J. M., & Foege, W. H. (1993). Actual causes of death in the United States. *Journal of the American Medical Association, 270*, 2207-2212.

McKennell, A. C., & Thomas, R. K. (1967). *Adults' and adolescents' smoking habits and attitudes.* London: Government Social Survey, HMSO.

McNeill, A. D. (1991). The development of dependence on smoking in children. *British Journal of Addiction, 86*, 589-592.

McNeill, A. D., Jarvis, M. J., Stapleton, J. A., West, R. J., & Bryant, A. (1989). Nicotine intake in young smokers: longitudinal study of saliva cotinine concentrations. *America Journal of Public Health, 79*, 172-175.

McNeill, A. D., Jarvis, M. J., & West, R. J. (1987). Subjective effects of cigarette smoking in adolescents. *Psychopharmacology, 92*, 115-117.

McNeill, A. D., West, R. J., Jarvis, M. J., Jackson, P., & Russell, M. A. H. (1986). Cigarette withdrawal symptoms in adolescent smokers. *Psychopharmacology, 92*, 533-536.

Mosbach, P., & Leventhal, H. (1988). Peer group identification and smoking: Implications for intervention. *Journal of Abnormal Psychology, 97*, 238-245.

Nelson, D. E., Giovino, G. A., Shopland, D. R., Mowery, P. D., Mills, S. L., & Eriksen, M. P. (1995). Trends in cigarette smoking among US adolescents, 1974 through 1991. *American Journal of Public Health, 85*, 34-40.

Noland, M. P., Kryscio, R. J., Riggs, R. S., Linville, L. H., Perritt, L. J., & Tucker, T. C. (1988). Saliva cotinine and thiocyanate: Chemical indicators of smokeless tobacco and cigarette use in adolescents. *Journal of Behavioral Medicine, 11*, 423-433.

Owen, N., Kent, P., Wakefield, M., & Roberts, L. (1995). Low-rate smokers. *Preventive Medicine, 24*, 80-84.

Pallonen, U. E., Prochaska, J. O., Velicer, W. F., Prokhorov, A. V., & Smith, N. F. (1998). Stages of acquisition and cessation for adolescent smoking: An empirical integration. *Addictive Behaviors, 23*, 303-324.

Parrott, A. (1994). Does cigarette smoking increase stress? *Addiction, 89*, 142-144.

Pechacek, T. F., Murray, D. M., Luepker, R. V., Mittelmark, M. B., Johnson, C. A., & Shutz, J. M. (1984). Measurement of adolescent smoking behavior: Rationale and methods. *Journal of Behavioral Medicine, 7*, 123-140.

Pierce, J. P., & Gilpin, E. (1996). How long will today's new adolescent smoker be addicted to cigarettes? *American Journal of Public Health, 86*, 253-256.

Pomerleau, O. F., Collins, A. C., Shiffman, S., & Pomerleau, C. S. (1993). Why some people smoke and others do not: New perspectives. *Journal of Consulting and Clinical Psychology, 61*, 723-731.

Prokhorov, A. V., Emmons, K. M., Pallonen, U. E., & Tsoh, J. Y. (1996a). Respiratory response to cigarette smoking among adolescent smokers: A pilot study. *Preventive Medicine, 25*, 633-640.

Prokhorov, A. V., Pallonen, U. E., Fava, J. L., Ding, L., & Niaura, R. (1996b). Measuring nicotine dependence among high-risk adolescent smokers. *Addictive Behaviors, 21*, 117-127.

Robinson, J. H., & Pritchard, W. S. (1992). The role of nicotine in tobacco use. *Psychopharmacology, 108*, 397-407.

Robinson, L. A., Klesges, R. C., Zbikowski, S. M., & Glaser, R. (1997). Predictors of risk for different stages of adolescent smoking in a biracial sample. *Journal of Consulting and Clinical Psychology, 65*, 653-662.

Rojas, N. L., Killen, J. D., Haydel, F., & Robinson, T. H. (1998). Nicotine dependence among adolescent smokers. *Archives of Pediatric and Adolescent Medicine, 152*, 151-156.

Russell, M. A. H. (1971). Cigarette smoking: Natural history of a dependence disorder. *British Journal of Medical Psychology, 44*, 1-16.

Russell, M. A. H. (1990). The nicotine addiction trap: A 40-year sentence for four cigarettes. *British Journal of Addiction, 85*, 293-300.

Russell, M. A. H., Peto, J., & Patel, U. A. (1978). The classification of smoking by factorial structure of motives. *Journal of the Royal Statistical Society Series A, 137*, 313-333.

Sargent, J. D., Mott, L. A., & Stevens, M. (1998). Predictors of smoking cessation in adolescents. *Archives of Pediatric and Adolescent Medicine, 152*, 388-393.

Shiffman, S. (1989). Tobacco "chippers"–individual differences in tobacco dependence. *Psychopharmacology, 97*, 539-547.

Shiffman, S. (1991). Refining models of dependence: Variations across persons and situations. *British Journal of Addiction, 86*, 611-615.

Shiffman, S. (1995). Comments on nicotine addiction. *Psychopharmacology, 117*, 14-15.

Shiffman, S., Hickcox, M., Paty, J. A., Gnys, M., Kassel, J. D., & Richards, T. (1996b). Progression from a smoking lapse to relapse: Prediction from abstinence violation effects, nicotine dependence, and lapse characteristics. *Journal of Consulting and Clinical Psychology, 64*, 993-1002.

Shiffman, S., Kassel, J. D., Paty, J., Gnys, M., & Zettler-Segal, M. (1994b). Smoking typology profiles of chippers and regular smokers. *Journal of Substance Abuse, 6*, 21-35.

Shiffman, S., Paty, J. A., Kassel, J. D., Gnys, M., & Zettler-Segal, M. (1994a). Smoking behavior and smoking history of tobacco chippers. *Experimental and Clinical Psychopharmacology, 2*, 126-142.

Shiffman, S., Hickcox, M., Gnys, M., Paty, J. A., & Kassel, J. D. (March, 1995a). *The nicotine dependence syndrome scale: Development of a new measure.* Paper presented at the Society for Research on Nicotine and Tobacco, San Diego, CA.

Shiffman, S., Paty, J. A., Gnys, M., Elash, C., & Kassel, J. D. (1995b). Nicotine withdrawal in chippers and regular smokers: Subjective and cognitive effects. *Health Psychology, 14*, 301-309.

Shiffman, S., Paty, J. A., Gnys, M., Kassel, J. D., & Hickcox, M. (1996a). First lapses to smoking: Within-subjects analysis of real-time reports. *Journal of Consulting and Clinical Psychology, 64*, 366-379.

Stanton, W. R. (1995). DSM-III-R tobacco dependence and quitting during late adolescence. *Addictive Behaviors, 20*, 595-603.

Tate, J. C., & Schmitz, J. M. (1993). A proposed revision of the Fagerstrom tolerance questionnaire. *Addictive Behaviors, 18*, 135-143.

U.S. Surgeon General (1989). *Reducing the health consequences of smoking: 25 years of progress.* Washington, D.C.: U.S. Government Printing Office.

U.S. Surgeon General (1994). *Preventing tobacco use among young people.* Washington, DC: U.S. Government Printing Office.

Wang, M. Q., Fitzhugh, E. C., Eddy, J. M., Fu, Q., & Turner, L. (1997). Social influences on adolescents' smoking progress: A longitudinal analysis. *American Journal of Health Behavior, 21*, 111-117.

West, R. (1993). Beneficial effects of nicotine: Fact or fiction? *Addiction, 88*, 589-590.

A Critical Evaluation
of Nicotine Replacement Therapy
for Teenage Smokers

Christi A. Patten

SUMMARY. The purpose of this review is to evaluate the appropriateness and feasibility of nicotine replacement therapy (NRT) in teenage smokers. In this paper, available forms of NRT, the theoretical rationale and efficacy of NRT, ethical considerations, and the feasibility of NRT in teenage smokers are addressed. Although there is a need to better understand the addiction process in adolescents, it is clear that teens have several characteristics similar to adult nicotine dependent smokers. These observations form the basis of the rationale for the use of NRT in teenagers. Only one report has examined the efficacy of NRT in teen smokers. This study observed a stop rate of 4.5% at six-months in 22 subjects using the nicotine patch. In addition to the potential benefits of NRT, ethical issues have been raised regarding the appropriate use of NRT in teenage smokers. Ethical considerations of NRT use in adult smokers, which need further study in adolescents, are nicotine absorption, long-term use, potential for side effects, concomitant smoking, use in pregnant smokers, and abuse liability in nonsmokers and light, intermittent smokers. The feasibility of NRT in adolescent smokers is also

Christi A. Patten is affiliated with Department of Psychology, Mayo Clinic, Rochester, MN.

Address correspondence to: Christi A. Patten, PhD, Assistant Professor of Psychology, Mayo Clinic, 200 First Street SW, Rochester, MN 55905 (E-mail: patten.christi@mayo.edu).

The author would like to acknowledge Lisa Sanderson-Cox, PhD, and Gary Croghan, MD, Mayo Clinic, for their critical and helpful reviews of an earlier draft of the manuscript.

[Haworth co-indexing entry note]: "A Critical Evaluation of Nicotine Replacement Therapy for Teenage Smokers." Patten, Christi A. Co-published simultaneously in *Journal of Child & Adolescent Substance Abuse* (The Haworth Press, Inc.) Vol. 9, No. 4, 2000, pp. 51-75; and: *Nicotine Addiction Among Adolescents* (ed: Eric F. Wagner) The Haworth Press, Inc., 2000, pp. 51-75. Single or multiple copies of this article are available for a fee from The Haworth Document Delivery Service [1-800-342-9678, 9:00 a.m. - 5:00 p.m. (EST). E-mail address: getinfo@haworthpressinc.com].

discussed, including its acceptability, convenience, social approval, cost, and availability. Many teens are nicotine dependent and additional clinical trials are warranted to evaluate whether NRT provides benefit to adolescent smokers. In addition, further research is needed to study adjunctive behavioral interventions tailored to the developmental and psychosocial needs of adolescents. *[Article copies available for a fee from The Haworth Document Delivery Service: 1-800-342-9678. E-mail address: <getinfo@haworthpressinc.com> Website: <http://www.haworthpressinc.com>]*

KEYWORDS. Smoking, adolescence, nicotine replacement

Cigarette smoking is the single most preventable cause of morbidity and mortality in the United States (McGinnis & Foerge, 1993). A considerable decline in the prevalence of smoking among American adults (Centers for Disease Control and Prevention [CDC], 1994a) has been blunted by a recent increase in smoking prevalence among adolescents (Glynn, Anderson, & Schwartz, 1991; CDC, 1998). More than 3,000 adolescents in the United States begin to use tobacco every day (Glynn et al., 1991). In 1991, 27% of teenagers in grades 9-12 had smoked cigarettes within the previous 30 days, and by 1997 the proportion had increased to 36% (CDC, 1998). The increasing trend in smoking prevalence occurred among all racial and ethnic subgroups. If current smoking patterns persist among adolescents, the public health burden of smoking will become even greater (CDC, 1996), thus underscoring the need for intensifying intervention efforts.

Adverse health consequences of smoking, including changes in pulmonary function and lipid proteins, bronchitis, and dyspnea on exertion have been demonstrated even among adolescent smokers (Dywer et al., 1988; Myers & Brown, 1994; US DHHS, 1984). Moreover, cigarette smoking among pregnant teenagers increases the risk of perinatal and infant death as well as other complications during pregnancy, including fetal growth retardation, premature birth, and low birth weight (Guyer, Strobino, Ventura, & Singh, 1995; Scholl & Salmon, 1986).

Very little work has been done to provide intervention for teen smokers. A recent review examined the available literature on the treatment of smoking among adolescents (Sussman, Lichtman, Ritt, & Pallonen, 1998a). In the 17 cessation studies reviewed, the program contents were derived from a wide range of theoretical perspectives, reflecting the early stage of research on adolescent smoking cessation. The end of treatment stop rate reported in 12 of the 17 studies averaged 20.7%, while the abstinence rate at three- to six-month follow-up dropped to a mean of 13%. This rate is only slightly higher than the estimates of the natural history of smoking cessation in adolescents which range from 0% to 11% over a six-month period (Moss, Allen, & Giovino,

1992; Sussman et al., 1998b). In addition, most studies were subject to a number of methodological limitations including use of a single group or quasi-experimental design and small sample sizes.

Smoking cessation programs with demonstrated effectiveness in adolescents are conspicuously absent from the literature (for an exception, see Myers, Brown, & Kelly, this publication). It is possible, however, to assess effective smoking interventions for adults and consider their feasibility for use in adolescent smoking cessation. The purpose of this review is to evaluate the appropriateness and feasibility of nicotine replacement therapy (NRT) for teenage smokers. Recent guidelines for the treatment of adult smokers recommend NRT as first line therapies (APA, 1996; Fiore et al., 1996). In this paper, available forms of NRT, the theoretical rationale and efficacy of NRT, ethical considerations, and the feasibility of NRT in teenage smokers are addressed.

NICOTINE REPLACEMENT THERAPIES

Four nicotine replacement therapies are FDA approved and available as aids to smoking cessation: the nicotine patch, nicotine gum, nicotine inhaler and the nicotine nasal spray. The *transdermal nicotine patch* delivers steady levels of nicotine through the skin (Hurt, Lauger, Offord, Kottke, & Dale, 1990). Doses typically range from 7 to 21 mg/day. Higher patch doses (e.g., 35 mg to 42 mg) have also been studied where smokers wear more than one patch at a time (Dale et al., 1995). The recommended duration of patch therapy is 6 to 12 weeks. After 4 to 6 weeks, individuals are usually tapered to lower doses, but most studies indicate tapering of the patch may not be necessary (Fiore, Smith, Jorenby, & Baker, 1994).

Nicotine polacrilex gum is administered ad-lib; the gum is chewed and then "parked" along the lining of the cheek for 20 to 30 minutes (Hughes, 1996). The recommended dose is 9 pieces of 2 mg gum per day for 3 months, which is then tapered over a maximum of 6 months. Nicotine gum is also available in 4 mg doses.

The nicotine inhaler is the newest nicotine replacement product to receive FDA approval (Tonnesen, Norregaard, Mikkelsen, Jorgensen, & Nilsson, 1993). This device is actually a puffer which looks similar to a cigarette holder. The cartridge produces a nicotine vapor when warm air is passed through it. The inhaler is used ad-lib for about 3 months, with a maximum duration of 6 months. The recommended minimum dose is 6, 4-mg cartridges per day, with a maximum of 16 cartridges/day (APA, 1996).

The nicotine nasal spray is a nicotine solution in a nasal spray bottle similar to those used with antihistamines (Sutherland et al., 1992a). The spray is used on an ad-lib basis and each dose (two sprays, one in each nostril) consists of 1 mg of nicotine. The recommended minimum dosing for the spray is 8 mg/day, with a maximum of 40 times/day, and the recommended duration is for up to 12 weeks. The spray can be tapered or stopped abruptly (Hurt et al., 1998).

CONCEPTUAL BASIS FOR NICOTINE REPLACEMENT THERAPY IN TEENAGE SMOKERS

Theoretical Model

Nicotine dependence is the basis for the use of NRT in adults (Benowitz, 1993). Individuals smoke primarily to obtain the desired reinforcing effects of nicotine including stimulation and relaxation, as well as relief of anxiety or depression. The most prominent adverse behavioral effect of nicotine is dependence (US DHHS, 1988). Although definitions of dependence vary, indicators of dependence include: (a) 20 or more cigarettes smoked per day, (b) elevated scores on the Fagerstrom Test for Nicotine Dependence, (c) withdrawal symptoms during stop attempts, and (d) continued use despite health consequences (Dale, Hurt, & Hays, 1998). Pharmacological-based theories of smoking emphasize the significance of physiological dependence in the maintenance of smoking behavior (Benowitz, 1983; Gilman, Goodman, Rall, & Murad, 1985). The underlying basis for the benefits of NRT is the mitigation of withdrawal symptoms which facilitates behavioral changes necessary for continued abstinence from smoking (Hughes, 1993a). Nicotine replacement may also directly suppress cigarette smoking by blunting the primary reinforcing effects of nicotine (Rose & Corrigall, 1997).

The evidence from adult studies supports pharmacological models of smoking cessation. The AHCPR guidelines, the most comprehensive recommendations for smoking cessation treatment to date, indicate that all forms of NRT show a doubling or tripling of the stop rate compared to placebo (Fiore et al., 1996). In addition, high dose patch therapy or combinations of NRT, such as the patch plus gum, enhance the rates of initial abstinence from smoking (Kornitzer, Boutsen, Dramaix, Thijs, & Gustavsson, 1995; Dale et al., 1995).

Behavioral therapy may be necessary for optimal benefit from NRT in adults. The gum, inhaler and spray are more effective in combination with behavioral counseling than with minimal (e.g., self-help) intervention (Hughes, 1991, Sutherland et al., 1992a; Hjalmarson, Franzon, Westin, & Wiklund, 1994; Schneider et al., 1995). Although the patch results in a doubling of the stop rate with minimal intervention (Tonnesen, Norregaard, Simonsen, & Sawe, 1991; Hays et al., 1998), the absolute long-term cessation rates are enhanced when it is combined with intensive behavioral counseling (Fiore et al., 1994). Even with the best combination of NRT and behavior therapy in adults, however, over 70% do not achieve long-term abstinence from smoking (Benowitz, 1993).

Nicotine replacement therapies are effective in mitigating withdrawal symptoms during smoking abstinence (Hughes, Higgins, & Hatsukami, 1990). Depending on the type of NRT, however, withdrawal symptoms are decreased selectively and some withdrawal symptoms, such as insomnia, hunger, and weight gain may not be alleviated at all (Hughes & Hatsukami, 1992). Interestingly, though replacement therapies do provide relief from most nicotine withdrawal symptoms, their effectiveness does not appear to be entirely due to this mechanism (Patten & Martin, 1996).

Nicotine Dependence in Adolescents

Nicotine dependence has been termed a pediatric disease (Kessler, 1995). It is now clear that the development of nicotine addiction typically occurs during adolescence (US DHHS, 1994), and children are becoming addicted at younger ages (Kandel, Chen, Warner, Kessler, & Grant, 1997). Among adult smokers, 70% were daily smokers before the age of 18 and 60% before the age of 14 (Glynn, Greenwald, Mills, & Manley, 1993; US DHHS, 1994). Approximately one-third of those experimenting with cigarettes during adolescence develop nicotine dependence (Anthony, Warner, & Kessler, 1994).

The Fagerstrom Test for Nicotine Dependence has been used in adolescent smokers and the scores have been in the range seen among adult addicted smokers with smoking rates comparable to the adolescent smokers (Kassel, this publication; Prokhorov, Pallonen, Fava, Ding, & Niaura, 1996; Rojas, Killen, Haydel, & Robinson, 1998). Adolescent smokers exhibit withdrawal symptoms when they try to stop smoking (McNeil, West, Jarvis, Jackson, & Bryant, 1986; Smith et al., 1996; Stanton, Lowe, & Silva, 1995) and nicotine craving is the most frequently reported symptom experienced during cessation (Dozois et al., 1995; Rojas et al., 1998).

When use of cigarettes progresses beyond initial experimentation, teens are likely to report various problems related to addiction and physical dependence (Henningfield, Clayton, & Pollin, 1990). The most frequent reasons that adolescents report for beginning to smoke are curiosity and social pressure (Pederson et al., 1997). However, adolescents who become regular smokers indicate that the important reasons for continuing to smoke are addiction/habit, pleasure, and reduction of negative affect (CDC, 1994b; Sarason et al., 1992; Stone & Kristeller, 1992; USDHHS, 1987).

A recent investigation (Sargent, Mott, & Stevens, 1998) examined factors associated with smoking cessation over a three-year period in 1,384 adolescents aged 12 to 18. Baseline predictors of smoking abstinence at follow-up were fewer cigarettes smoked per day and fewer prior quit attempts. For example, the rate of smoking cessation was 46.3% among 123 occasional smokers compared to 6.8% among 88 teens who smoked 10 or more cigarettes per day. Moreover, studies which included smokers aged 16 to 20 years indicate that level of nicotine dependence has a greater influence on cessation than such variables as age and gender (Kottke et al., 1992).

Approximately 70% of adolescent smokers report that they desire to quit smoking and indicate that they would not have started smoking if they could choose again (George, 1992). Moreover, three of four younger smokers have tried unsuccessfully to stop smoking at least once (Moss et al., 1992; Dozois et al., 1995). While adolescent smokers realize the negative health consequences associated with smoking, most express little concern for their personal well-being (Dappen, Schwartz, & O'Donnell, 1996). However, those teen smokers who are successful in stopping smoking report that personal concern about the health consequences of tobacco use is an important motivator (Dozois et al., 1995; Rose, Chassin, Presson, & Sherman, 1996).

Thus, research supports the premise that nicotine dependence plays an important role in the persistence of smoking in adolescents. Although there is a need to better understand the addiction process in adolescents, it is clear that teens have several characteristics similar to adult, nicotine dependent smokers. Teenage smokers develop nicotine dependence, experience withdrawal symptoms, smoke for negative affect reduction, continue to smoke despite negative health consequences, and have difficulty in stopping smoking. These observations form the basis of the rationale for the use of NRT in teenagers. A recent CDC workgroup on youth cessation (Sussman, 1997) recommended that treatments that work in adults, including NRT, should be evaluated in adolescents. Therefore, the pharmacological model using the nicotine patch, gum, inhaler and spray may be useful in nicotine dependent adolescents.

Efficacy of NRT in Adolescents

Unfortunately, no randomized clinical trials of NRT in adolescents under the age of 18 have been conducted. One study of nicotine patch therapy was reported in 22 adolescents aged 13 to 17 (Smith et al., 1996). At baseline, the adolescents smoked an average of 23.3 cigarettes per day, their mean Fagerstrom score was 7.2, and 73% had other smokers living in their household. Results of the Aschenbach Child Behavior Checklist indicated that the adolescents showed significant adverse deviation from the normative mean in many of the categories, such as being withdrawn, having somatic complaints, being anxious and/or depressed, and having delinquent and aggressive behavior.

The duration of open-label nicotine patch therapy was for 8 weeks (22 mg/d for six weeks and 11 mg/d for two weeks). The subjects also participated in one-hour, weekly group sessions and individual behavioral counseling throughout the treatment phase. The behavioral intervention was adapted from an adult model of smoking cessation.

Eighteen (82%) of the 22 experienced at least one adverse medication event during the 8-week treatment phase and 15 (68%) reported some type of skin reaction. Additional side effects reported were headache, nausea and vomiting, tiredness, dizziness and arm pain. The frequency of occurrence of side effects were similar to that reported in studies of adults who wore a 22 mg/d patch. For all adverse events, there was no episode of more than moderate intensity and none led to the discontinuation of patch therapy. Thus, it was concluded that patch therapy seemed safe and well-tolerated by adolescent smokers.

At the end of treatment and 6-month follow-up, the biochemically confirmed smoking abstinence rates were 14% and 4.5%, respectively. The mean number of cigarettes smoked per day dropped throughout the treatment phase, but these changes were not maintained during the follow-up period. There was also a significant decrease in withdrawal symptom scores for adolescents over the treatment phase.

This study indicates that, unlike adults, nicotine patch therapy plus group support is not effective in adolescents. The reasons for the disappointingly low stop rates in adolescents using the nicotine patch are unclear. Although the subjects experienced withdrawal symptom relief, there was no apparent benefit in terms of cessation. This finding is similar to adults where withdrawal severity is not related to smoking cessation outcomes (Patten & Martin, 1996). There was a high frequency of side effects and the experience of these adverse events could have decreased the potential efficacy of the patch. However, the side effects were no worse than those observed in adults and none of the adolescents discontinued the study because of side effects. It is also possible that the adolescents were not compliant with use of the patch, thereby limiting its utility. To address this issue, the author examined unpublished data collected in this study and found excellent rates of adherence to the treatment protocol with respect to attendance, self-monitoring, and patch use. Attendance at the 10 visits during the nicotine patch phase averaged 91% (SD = 5, range 86% to 100%), and compliance with self-monitoring of patch use averaged 50 of 56 possible days (SD = 12, range 3 to 56). Based on the daily self-monitoring data, 83% of subjects reported that the patch was worn all or part of the time over the 56 days of treatment. Thus, the lack of patch efficacy does not appear to be due to poor compliance.

Alternatively, the observation of poorer results for nicotine patch therapy may suggest that adolescents respond differently to pharmacological approaches than adults. Adolescents may smoke for different reasons than adults and pharmacological interventions that focus on reducing withdrawal or the reinforcing effects of nicotine may be less effective in adolescents. Adolescents may require NRT to treat the physical dependence on nicotine, but the cessation process might be different behaviorally for teens, compared with adults, because of the unique characteristics of this age group that include a high sensitivity to peer, parental and other environmental influences (Chassin, Presson, Sherman, & Edwards, 1991). The group based support provided to the subjects was based on an adult model of cessation and was not tailored to the needs of the adolescents. An adult model of smoking cessation may simply not work in adolescents. It is important to learn more about the specific needs of adolescent smokers in order to develop effective treatments. Methods of smoking cessation used for adults may prove to be effective with adolescents, if given in a developmentally appropriate fashion (Hollis et al., 1994).

There are no reports of the use of nicotine gum, inhaler, or spray in adolescents. Treatments that are effective for one route of tobacco administration may not generalize to others. Because many adolescents are nicotine dependent, further clinical trials using NRT are warranted to clearly evaluate whether NRT will benefit adolescent smokers. In addition to the potential efficacy of NRT, researchers and clinicians alike are confronted with ethical issues regarding the appropriate use of NRT in teen smokers.

ETHICAL CONSIDERATIONS IN USE OF NICOTINE REPLACEMENT THERAPY IN TEENAGE SMOKERS

Concerns have been raised in the literature regarding the use of NRT in both adult and adolescent smokers (Mitchell, 1997). These concerns focus on the dependence potential and safety of NRT. Many smokers as well as clinicians believe that nicotine is dangerous and that NRT should be avoided (Benowitz, 1997). Several considerations of the risks of NRT in adults are reviewed in detail elsewhere (Benowitz, Porchet, Sheiner, & Jacob, 1988; Henningfield, & Keenan, 1993; Hughes, 1993b). These include nicotine absorption, long-term use, side effects, concomitant smoking, use among pregnant or nursing females, and abuse liability in nonsmokers and non-dependent smokers. These variables can also be considered in determining whether the potential risks of NRT outweigh the possible benefits in adolescent smokers.

Nicotine Absorption and Replacement Levels

The potential for dependence on NRT is related to the rate and amount of nicotine absorption by the body (Benowitz, 1997). Cigarette smoking delivers nicotine to the brain within 10 seconds after inhalation, which is faster than any other route of administration (Slade, 1993) and produces immediate reinforcing effects (Rose & Corrigall, 1997). The effects of nicotine are greater when doses are administered rapidly compared with when the same dose is given more slowly (Benowitz, 1991).

Different forms of NRT produce different rates and amount of nicotine absorption in adults. The nicotine in patches is slowly absorbed so that on the first day nicotine blood levels peak 6 to 10 hours after patch application. The nicotine levels obtained with patch use are about half those obtained by cigarette smoking (Palmer & Faulds, 1992). The nicotine in gum is also absorbed gradually through the lining of the mouth, with peak absorption occurring after 20 to 30 minutes of use. Much of the nicotine is retained in the gum though improper chewing or swallowing of the gum (Hughes & Glaser, 1993; Fiore et al., 1992). Thus, ad-lib use of the 2 mg or 4 mg gum produces nicotine concentrations of about 30% to 50% of those from smoking ciga- rettes (McNabb, Ebert, & McCusker, 1982). Nicotine absorption with the inhaler also occurs relatively slowly, primarily through the lining of the mouth (Lunell et al., 1995). Peak nicotine blood levels are obtained approxi- mately 10-15 minutes after the end of puffing and the nicotine replacement levels are about one-third of those of cigarette smoking. The spray provides the fastest delivery system of any currently available NRT product (Sutherland et al., 1992b). Peak absorption occurs within 10 minutes (Hughes & Glaser, 1993). The prompt alleviation of withdrawal symptoms may contribute to its reinforcing effect and dependence potential (Hurt et al., 1998). With repeated doses and during ad-lib use, blood nicotine concentrations can be maintained at smoking levels. Technique of use is important, however, and nicotine ab- sorption varies widely among subjects. Thus, the levels of nicotine replace- ment obtained with the spray are approximately 40% to 60% of those of cigarette smoking (Sutherland et al., 1992b).

Based on the data on nicotine absorption in adults, the risk of dependence in adolescents is expected to be greatest with the spray and least with the patch. However, several studies in adults suggest that all forms of NRT are likely to produce substantially lower risk than cigarette smoking in adoles- cents. First, the slower release of nicotine with the patches, gum and inhaler results in lower peak blood nicotine concentrations and does not produce the positively reinforcing effects reported by cigarette smokers (Benowitz, 1993). Although the nasal spray does have the potential of allowing more direct substitution of nicotine dosing (Benowitz, 1993), the speed of absorp- tion with all forms of NRT is much less than that of cigarette smoking. Secondly, in contrast to cigarette smoking, NRT does not produce tar or carbon monoxide, the substances most directly associated with cancer and cardiovascular disease risks of smoking (Benowitz, 1991; Hughes & Glaser, 1993; US DHHS, 1990).

It is important to note that research in adolescents examining nicotine absorption from cigarettes and NRT is sparse. For example, there may be variation in nicotine metabolism among teens related to differences in nicotine absorption and distribution and differences in the duration of inhalation of smoking (Ahijevych, 1998). The Smith et al. (1996) study reported lower blood cotinine levels at baseline than those in adults with comparable smoking rates, but the authors speculated overreporting of the smoking rate by adolescents as one explanation for the differences. In addition, at weeks 4 and 8 when adolescents were wearing the 22 mg/d and 11 mg/d patch, respectively, the blood cotinine levels were higher than baseline levels, but not significantly different than those in adults in a previous study administered the same patch dose.

Long-Term Use

Concerns have been raised regarding long-term use, or prolonged dependence on NRT. Cigarette smoking occurs frequently and in response to stressful situations; smokers self-administer about 200 times per day (APA, 1996). The patch may help to break the association between nicotine and environmental situations because nicotine is delivered independent of these events (Hughes & Glaser, 1993). Indeed, long-term use or dependence on the patch in adults has not been reported (Fiore et al., 1992). Conversely, ad-lib use of the gum, inhaler and spray continues the conditioning of nicotine intake with relief from withdrawal and stressful situations and may contribute to long term use. About 10-20% of adults who stop smoking with nicotine gum continue use for 9 or more months, but few use the gum longer than 2 years (Hughes, 1991). Studies suggest that most long term use may reflect an effective strategy for maintaining abstinence rather than dependence (APA, 1996). For example, all but 1-2% of smokers eventually stop gum use and the amount of gum use at long-term follow-up is minimal (usually less than 12 mg/d) (Hughes, 1991). Long-term use of the inhaler has not been evaluated beyond 6 months in clinical trials with adults. The insert for the Nicotrol® nasal spray (1996) indicates that 15%-20% of adults use the spray beyond the recommended duration for 6 to 12 months. In addition, dependence on the spray was reported by 32% of active spray users and 13% of placebo users. Conversely, Hurt et al. (1998) instructed subjects to taper the spray and limited its availability to subjects after the treatment phase. A progressive decline in the mean daily frequency of spray use was observed from 15.0 doses during week 1 to 7.5 doses during week 8. The number of days between the first and last spray use was 49.8 (range 5 to 57). Thus, extended use of NRT may be affected by instructions and availability.

In teenagers, the use of NRT in the form of gum, inhaler or spray without concurrent behavioral therapy may not only contribute to prolonged dependence on NRT but may diminish the adolescent's opportunities to learn alternative coping skills in response to stressful situations and negative emotions. Studies suggest that the psychological function of regulating negative affect is a motive for cigarette use in adolescents (Wills, McNamara, Vaccaro, & Hirky, 1996). A substantial proportion of adolescents report smoking to reduce stress and negative affect (CDC, 1994b). Teens may also lack alternative coping resources for dealing with stressful situations without smoking (Wills et al., 1996). Thus, prolonged NRT use could be detrimental to the long-term development of the adolescent's coping repertoire.

Side Effects

A major consideration is whether NRT is safe for use in adolescents. Further research is needed in adolescents on the safety of various doses of the patch, and side effects associated with the gum, inhaler and spray.

Recent clinical trials and experimental studies suggest that nicotine patches and gum do not have clinically significant adverse cardiovascular effects in adults, even in those with cardiovascular disease who continue to smoke (Benowitz & Gourlay, 1997; Hughes & Glaser, 1993). Adolescents using the patch showed similar side effects as in adult smokers (Smith et al., 1996) including skin irritation (e.g., itching), erythma at the site of the patch, insomnia and nausea (Hurt et al., 1990). Contraindications to patch use include dermatoses and history of severe skin reactions. Adverse effects of the nicotine gum in adults are mouth, throat and stomach irritation, hiccups, sore jaw, air swallowing, and loss of dental fillings (Fagerstrom, Schneider, & Lunell, 1993). Thus, the gum is inappropriate for those with dental problems. Side effects of the inhaler in adults include indigestion, coughing, mouth and throat irritation, hiccups, unpleasant taste, indigestion, and dizziness (Nicotrol® Inhaler Insert, 1997). Contraindications to its use include pregnancy or nursing females, and asthma. Finally, use of the spray is associated with nasal irritation, rhinitis, sneezing, throat irritation, coughing, and watering eyes which decline with usage (Hjalmarson et al., 1994; Hurt et al., 1998; Schneider et al., 1995). The spray is not indicated in those with chronic nasal disorder, asthma, active chemical dependence on alcohol/drugs, psychiatric disorders, use of other medications or in pregnant or nursing females (Benowitz, 1997; Hurt et al., 1998).

It is well documented that screening for medical contraindications and instructions on proper use decrease the potential for side effects. One concern regarding NRT use in adolescents is the over-the-counter availability of the gum and some forms of the nicotine patch. Although adolescents must be over the age of 18 or have a parent present to purchase over the counter NRT, pharmacies and drug stores may vary in terms of their consistency in enforc-ing these mandates. To address this issue, I conducted an informal survey of 25 drugstores in Rochester, MN and asked the pharmacists whether teenagers under the age of 18 could purchase nicotine gum or patches on their own, without the presence of a parent or legal guardian. Interestingly, 11 of 25 (44%) answered affirmatively, stating that teens could purchase the products on their own, 12 reported that minors could not purchase these products without the presence of a parent/guardian, and 2 were unsure. Several of the 12 who reported that teens could not purchase NRT on their own commented that they were concerned that minors would "try nicotine and become ad-dicted," or "get addicted to these products." These results indicate that some minors may be able to purchase over-the-counter NRT on their own. The use of nicotine without physician advice and/or parental support is of concern as some adolescents may use the products improperly, have medical conditions that would prohibit their use, or be light, intermittent smokers, and thereby increase their risk of side effects.

Concomitant Smoking

Concern has been expressed that the combination of cigarette smoking and NRT may increase risk for nicotine toxicity (Benowitz & Gourlay, 1997). Adolescents who have difficulty stopping smoking or who have personality characteristics, such as sensation seeking or rebelliousness, may continue to smoke while on NRT (Pierce, Farkas, & Evans, 1993). Indeed, Smith et al. (1996) observed that 13 of the 22 adolescents continued to smoke while on patch therapy, with a range of 1 to 6 cigarettes smoked per day. At week 4, while receiving a 22 mg/d patch, the blood cotinine levels for all adolescent subjects was 197 ± 92 ng/ml, compared to 153 ± 80 ng/ml at baseline. When adjusting for concomitant smoking, the cotinine levels at week 4 were somewhat lower with a mean of 173 ± 91. The highest baseline cotinine level among the adolescents was 300 ng/ml and the highest cotinine level during the patch phase was 338 ng/ml without significant toxicity. In addi-tion, studies in adults of the cardiovascular effects of the combination of nicotine and cigarette smoking, suggest a flat dose response curve, whereby the total intake of nicotine is no more than modestly increased compared with that of smoking alone (Benowitz, 1997; Benowitz & Gourlay, 1997). Never-theless, NRT appears to be safe in adults who continue to smoke (Dale et al., 1995). However, further studies are needed to address the safety of concom-itant smoking during use of NRT in adolescents.

NRT During Pregnancy

Perhaps the most widely discussed ethical concern is the use of NRT in pregnant or nursing females. Many pregnant and nursing teenagers are nicotine dependent; 27% to 67% continue to smoke cigarettes throughout pregnancy, and most are heavy smokers (Bragg, 1997; Davis, Tollestrup, & Millham, 1990). Most of the harmful effects of smoking occur in the third trimester; thus cessation of smoking in the first or second trimester greatly reduces risk (Ershoff, Quinn, Mullen, Lairson, 1990). One study found that a behavioral smoking intervention which included a smoking teenage buddy was no more effective than usual care in pregnant teenagers (Albrecht, 1998). Thus, if pregnant or nursing nicotine dependent teens are unable to stop smoking on their own or with behavioral intervention, it seems appropriate to consider NRT in the form of patches or gum which have been found to be safe and effective in pregnant smoking adults (Hays et al., 1998; Oncken et al., 1997; Wright et al., 1997).

Several recent papers have concluded that the benefits of NRT in adult pregnant women, who cannot stop smoking without such therapy, substantially outweigh the risks of continued smoking or the potential risks of NRT (Benowitz, 1993; Slade, 1993). There is concern about the use of NRT in this group because nicotine may contribute to reproductive disturbances during pregnancy (Navarro et al., 1989; Benowitz, 1997). However, cigarette smoking not only delivers nicotine, but carbon monoxide and other toxic chemicals (Slade, 1993). Moreover, the level of nicotine to which the fetus is exposed is much lower from nicotine gum and patches relative to cigarettes, producing substantially lower risk (Benowitz, 1991). However, the inhaler and nicotine nasal spray have not been studied in pregnant or nursing females.

Use in Nonsmokers and Non-Dependent Smokers

The issue of experimentation with NRT is of relevance in nonsmoking teens who may try these products out of curiosity and/or rebelliousness. Concerns have been raised that teens may have access to over-the-counter nicotine patches and gum and that these products may serve as "gateway drugs." A recent study addressed this issue by conducting biannual school surveys, beginning in 1996, in a representative sample of 95,000 students in grades 7 to 12 (Adams & McGrath, 1998). Interestingly, the prevalence of experimentation with the nicotine patch was very low (less than 1%). There are no reports examining nicotine gum use among nonsmoking adolescents.

Studies suggest a subset of teens experiment but are not dependent on nicotine (Pierce et al., 1993). Thus, it is possible that NRT use could increase physical dependence, or the potential for dependence, in adolescents who are not nicotine dependent. However, occasional smokers may not be motivated to seek treatment. In light of current guidelines with adults, NRT does not appear to be ethically appropriate nor recommended for use in teenagers who are light, intermittent smokers.

Summary

Unfortunately, most of the data to inform risk-benefit decisions on the use of NRT in teenage smokers are based on adult samples. It is clear that many adolescents are nicotine dependent and that additional trials are needed to examine the efficacy of NRT. In addition to the benefits of NRT in adolescents, we need to learn more about nicotine absorption, side effects, concomitant smoking, and use in pregnant teens, nonsmokers, and non-dependent smokers. Preliminary studies in teenage smokers indicate that the findings may be similar to those in adults. For example, the side effect profile of the nicotine patch was similar in adolescents and adults (Smith et al., 1996). At this stage of the research, however, the benefits of NRT cannot be assumed. Until further studies are conducted, it is reasonable to conclude that NRT is not appropriate for adolescents who are light, intermittent smokers, pregnant smokers, and those with contraindications to NRT.

FEASIBILITY OF NICOTINE REPLACEMENT THERAPY IN TEENAGE SMOKERS

If NRT is shown to be effective and appropriate for use in adolescents, an important issue is whether NRT is feasible in this population. As with any type of smoking intervention evaluated for use in adolescents, we need to consider the acceptability, convenience, social approval, cost and availability of NRT.

Acceptability

One consideration is whether NRT is acceptable to adolescent smokers. Some adolescents may be uncomfortable with pharmacological treatment. Teens need to be informed of the possible side effects associated with NRT because these may not be tolerable. Adverse effects (e.g., insomnia) have the potential to interfere with the adolescent's performance at school, work, and sports, and may limit involvement in recreational and social activities. Some side effects are manageable and thus tolerable. For instance, the patch can be removed before bedtime to alleviate insomnia, and skin reactions can be treated with over-the-counter hydrocortisone cream. In addition, rotating patch sites (applying the patch to a different site on the body each day) helps to minimize local irritation. Interestingly, however, many adolescents in our patch studies reported that they did not have enough money to purchase hydrocortisone cream for skin reactions and samples were provided to several subjects free of charge. Thus, cost may be a barrier to effective management of side effects and may decrease the utility of NRT. In addition, teens may decide that the side effects of NRT are not worth the potential interference with daily activities.

NRT may be preferred by those teens not willing to attend formal behavioral programs such as group-based smoking cessation therapies. However, all forms of NRT will likely require at least some behavioral counseling on proper use to decrease the potential for side effects and to enhance compliance.

An additional consideration is the appeal of different forms of NRT. Our experience indicates that adolescents are easily recruited within a short time period to participate in trials of patch therapy. When asked why they are interested in participating, many state that they want to enroll because of the "free patches." However, it may be that any type of therapy that is offered free of charge would appeal to adolescents. The gum and spray may appeal to adolescents who desire a active means of coping with withdrawal symptoms, whereas the inhaler may work best for those who want the ritual, tactile, and sensory stimulation that this device may provide.

Convenience

The ease of administration of NRT may increase compliance and its acceptability in teen smokers. The patches are easy to administer and do not require active intervention by the adolescent after they are applied daily each morning (Fiore et al., 1992). There are no reported activity restrictions while using the patch (Fiore et al., 1996) which may increase its utility in adolescents. The dose can be tailored, though the dosing is less flexible than with other forms of NRT.

The nicotine gum, inhaler and spray are administered ad-lib; the dosing is flexible and can be tailored to the adolescent's needs. These products can be carried by the teen in a pocket, purse or small pouch. However, they require frequent use during the day to maintain adequate nicotine levels, which may be inconvenient and interfere with the adolescent's daily activities. For example, if the adolescent is playing a sport, he or she would need to interrupt the activity relatively frequently to use the inhaler. Of note, puffing on the inhaler must be done more frequently than puffing on a cigarette to maintain adequate nicotine levels. Moreover, nicotine gum use is somewhat restricted in that consumption of acidic beverages should be avoided immediately before, during and after gum use (Henningfield et al., 1993).

Compliance

Another consideration is the level of effort necessary to adhere to NRT and whether adolescents will comply. In adults, the patch is associated with few compliance problems that would interfere with its effective use. Preliminary data also suggest that adolescents show high levels of compliance with the nicotine patch (Smith et al., 1996). In adults, adherence with nicotine gum is much less than with the patch, whereas compliance with the inhaler and spray appear to be adequate. Additional research is needed to compare adherence rates across alternative forms of NRT in adolescents.

Social Acceptability

Another consideration is whether NRT is acceptable within the teen's peer groups and social environment. Excepting the nicotine patch, most forms of NRT are detectable to others. Consequently, the adolescent's use of NRT in social situations (e.g., dating, sports) may result in ridicule or embarrassment. The adolescent's use of an inhaler may be mistaken for a cigarette which could have negative consequences in many situations including school, work, and sports. The gum is generally undetectable to others but many schools prohibit gum use in the schools. Although teenage smokers have higher absenteeism and drop-out rates (Pirie, Murray, & Luepker, 1988), in 1996, only 6% of teens aged 16-17 years in the U.S. were not enrolled in a high school program and had not completed high school (CDC, 1998). Research indicates that the primary reasons adolescents attempt to stop smoking are sports participation and partners/friends (Dozois et al., 1995). Thus, the social acceptability of some forms of NRT may determine whether these are viable options for adolescent smokers.

Cost

The adolescent's economic concerns may also influence whether NRT is a practical treatment alternative. Many insurance companies do not assist with paying for smoking cessation programs. However, the high cost for disadvantaged, low SES adolescents and/or their parents may be offset by not buying cigarettes (Montalto & Garrett, 1998). Most of the costs for nicotine replacement are comparable to those of cigarette smoking. For example, the cost for a 12-week supply of NRT is approximately $350 for the patch, $322 for the 2-mg gum, $504 for the inhaler, and $393 for the spray. In comparison, the average cost of smoking 20 cigarettes per day for 12 weeks is $252.

Availability

A final consideration regarding use of NRT in adolescents is its availability. Whether NRT is purchased over-the-counter or with a prescription, parental/guardian consent will likely be needed. This raises issues of confidentiality, as some adolescents may fear that their parents will find out about their smoking. However, the results of Smith et al. (1996) and our ongoing nicotine patch trial with teen smokers indicate that parental consent is not a barrier to recruitment. In addition, one study revealed that only 13% of the parents did not know about the adolescent's smoking (Dozois et al., 1995).

The inhaler and spray and some forms of the patch are available only by a prescription. One disadvantage is that this will require access to health care, which may not be feasible for low SES adolescents and their families. However, adolescents attending school can receive a prescription from the school health clinic. Indeed, many schools mandate that any prescription drugs be provided by a school health care provider.

An important advantage to requiring a prescription for NRT is that physician and health care professional advice and follow-up will likely enhance its proper use and efficacy in teens, and decrease the potential for side effects. Adolescents purchasing NRT over the counter may not understand or may disregard package instructions, contributing to improper use. Physicians and other health care providers may have an important opportunity to reach a large number of adolescent smokers by providing NRT and advice to stop smoking. Studies show small but significant quit rates at one year among adult smokers receiving a brief office intervention for smoking cessation (Fiore et al., 1996).

Smoking cessation counseling provided by a physician or other health care provider may be as important as the availability of NRT (Eberman, Dale, & Patten, 1998). Results of youth focus groups conducted by the American Medical Association (AMA) (Balch, 1997) indicate that teens would accept help if they were assured that it would be confidential and would not be a lecture, and if the sessions were short. Aspects of smoking cessation advice that were perceived by the adolescents as negative were preaching and nagging. Moreover, teens would like to be involved in their own treatment decisions; they prefer to set their own progress and their own goals. These results should be considered when counseling adolescents to stop smoking.

FUTURE DIRECTIONS:
INTERVENTIONS TAILORED TO ADOLESCENTS

Although NRT is an important smoking cessation adjunct and should be studied in adolescents, researchers and clinicians need to think broadly about interventions offered to adolescents based on their developmental and psychosocial needs. Multiple levels of influence should be considered in interventions designed to treat adolescent smokers, including addiction, psychological, peer and parental influences (CDC, 1994b; Fiore et al., 1996). For example, interventions to enhance parental support for smoking cessation could be developed and then optimized when parents accompany adolescents to purchase over-the-counter NRT or to obtain a prescription from a health care provider. It may be premature to conclude that programs focused solely on the adolescent will not work. However, given the evidence thus far, it seems probable that a comprehensive and creative approach to smoking cessation among adolescents will be needed. The challenge is to design and test the configuration of pharmacologic and behavioral interventions that will result in high initial smoking cessation and avert relapse to smoking.

Recently, the AMA developed a brief office intervention for adolescent smokers (Levenberg & Elsterm, 1995) through a national advisory panel in the fields of nicotine dependence, adolescent medicine, health psychology, and teen focus groups. The intervention addresses the developmental and psychosocial needs of adolescents incorporating stage of change; peer, parental and other social influences; negative affect; addiction; and self-efficacy. The health care provider uses motivational interviewing combined with a youth centered, individualized clinical approach (Levenberg & Elsterm, 1995). The brief office intervention may be useful as an adjunct to NRT because it is tailored to adolescents.

Computer-based interventions also provide an opportunity to combine NRT with behavioral interventions tailored to adolescents (Pallonen et al., 1998). With funding through NCI, we are currently developing an Internet-based program which will be evaluated for in home use in teen smokers. The content for the intervention will be based on an assessment of the needs of adolescents. However, it is anticipated that information on NRT and other medications for smoking cessation will be provided. Although adolescents will be instructed to obtain a prescription from their physician if they request NRT or other medications for smoking cessation, they will have the opportunity to learn about the different medications and ask questions regarding their proper use, side effects, etc. through the computer linkage system. Internet-based treatment has the potential for widespread dissemination and avoids some of the barriers imposed by traditional behavioral interventions, such as geographic restrictions to clinics, time commitments, and cost.

CONCLUSION

This review highlights several gaps in our knowledge of adolescent smokers. Further study is needed to determine the risks, benefits, and feasibility of NRT in adolescents. Many adolescents are nicotine dependent and are at future risk of tobacco-related morbidity and mortality. Thus, clinical trials examining the efficacy of NRT in teens are clearly warranted. However, the efficacy of NRT in adolescents cannot be assumed and it is possible that its use may increase risk of dependence and adverse side effects. Moreover, NRT does not address the developmental and psychosocial factors which influence adolescent cessation. Therefore, it makes sense to examine the effectiveness of NRT in the context of behavioral interventions tailored to the needs of adolescents.

REFERENCES

Adams, E. H., & McGrath, P. (1998, August). Post-marketing surveillance of the Nicotrol® patch among school students. Presented at the Society for Research on Nicotine and Tobacco, Copenhagen, Denmark.

Ahijevych, K. (1998). Nicotine metabolism variability and nicotine addiction. In: Nicotine-individual risk factors for initiation. Addicted to nicotine: A national Research Forum. National Institute of Drug Abuse.

Albrecht, S. A. (1998 August). Short and long term effectiveness of smoking cessation in pregnant teens. Presented at the Society for Research on Nicotine and Tobacco, Copenhagen, Denmark.

American Psychiatric Association (APA). (1996). Practice guideline for the treatment of patients with nicotine dependence. *American Journal of Psychiatry, 153,* 1-25.

Anthony, J. C., Warner, L. A., & Kessler, R. C. (1994). Comparative epidemiology of dependence on tobacco, alcohol, controlled substances, and inhalants: Basic findings from the National Comorbidity Survey. *Experimental and Clinical Psychopharmacology, 2,* 244-268.

Balch, G. (1997, August). Youth focus groups on smoking cessation. CDC Youth Tobacco Use Cessation Meeting. Atlanta, Georgia.

Benowitz, N. L. (1983). Pharmacologic aspects of cigarette smoking and nicotine addiction. *New England Journal of Medicine, 19,* 1318-1330.

Benowitz, N. L. (1991). Nicotine replacement therapy during pregnancy. *The Journal of the American Medical Association, 266,* 3174-3177.

Benowitz, N. L. (1993). Nicotine replacement therapy. What has been accomplished–can we do better? *Drugs, 45,* 157-170.

Benowitz, N. L. (1997). Treating tobacco addiction–nicotine or no nicotine? *The New England Journal of Medicine, 337,* 1230-1231.

Benowitz, N. L., & Gourlay, S. G. (1997). Cardiovascular toxicity of nicotine: Implications for nicotine replacement therapy. *Journal of the American College of Cardiology, 29,* 1422-1431.

Benowitz, N. L., Porchet, H., Sheiner, L., Jacob, P., III. (1988). Nicotine absorption and cardiovascular effects with smokeless tobacco use: Comparison with cigarettes and nicotine gum. *Clinical Pharmacology and Therapeutics, 44,* 23-28.

Bragg, E. J. (1997). Pregnant adolescents with addictions. *Journal of Obstetric, Gynecologic, and Neonatal Nursing, 26,* 577-584.

Centers for Disease Control and Prevention (CDC). (1994a). Cigarette smoking among adults–United States, 1993. *Morbidity and Mortality Weekly Report, 43,* 925-930.

Centers for Disease Control and Prevention (CDC). (1994b). Reasons for tobacco use and symptoms of nicotine withdrawal among adolescent and young tobacco users–United States, 1993. *Morbidity and Mortality Weekly Report, 43*, 745-750.

Centers for Disease Control and Prevention (CDC). (1996). Projected smoking-related deaths among youth–United States. *Morbidity and Mortality Weekly Report, 45*, 971-974.

Centers for Disease Control and Prevention (CDC). (1998). Tobacco use among high school students–United States, 1997. *Morbidity and Mortality Weekly Report, 47*, 229-233.

Chassin, L., Presson, C. C., Sherman, S. J., & Edwards, D. A. (1991). Four pathways to young adult smoking status: Adolescent social-psychological antecedents in a midwestern community sample. *Health Psychology, 10*, 409-418.

Dale, L. C., Hurt, R. D., Hays, J. T. (1998, in press). Pharmacologic treatment of nicotine dependence. *Postgraduate Medicine*.

Dale, L. C., Hurt, R. D., Offord, K. P., Lawson, G. M., Croghan, I. T,. & Schroeder, D. R. (1995). High dose nicotine patch therapy: Percentage replacement and smoking cessation. *Journal of the American Medical Association, 274*, 1353-1358.

Dappen, A., Schwartz, R. H., & O'Donnell, R. (1996). A survey of adolescent smoking patterns. *Journal of the American Board of Family Practice, 9*, 7-13.

Davis, R. L., Tollestrup, K., & Milham, S., Jr. (1990). Trends in teenage smoking during pregnancy: Washington State, 1984-1988. *American Journal of Diseases of Children, 144*, 1297-1301.

Dozois, D. N., Farrow, J. A., & Miser, A. (1995). Smoking patterns and cessation motivations during adolescence. *International Journal of the Addictions, 30*, 1485-1498.

Dwyer, J. H., Rieger-Ndakorerwa, G. E., Semmer, N. K., Fuchs, R., & Lippert, P. (1988). Low level cigarette smoking and longitudinal change in serum cholesterol among adolescents. *Journal of the American Medical Association, 259*, 2857-2862.

Eberman, K., Dale, L., & Patten, C.A. (1998, in press). Methods for counseling patients for tobacco cessation. *Post Graduate Medicine*m

Ershoff, D. H., Quinn, V. P., Mullen, P. D., Lairson, D. R. (1990). Pregnancy and medical cost outcomes of a self-help prenatal smoking cessation program in a HMO. *Public Health Reports, 105*, 340-247.

Fagerstrom, K. O., Schneider, N. G., & Lunell, E. (1993). Effectiveness of nicotine patch and nicotine gum as individual versus combined treatments for tobacco withdrawal symptoms. *Psychopharmacology, 111*, 271-277.

Fiore, M. C., Bailey, W. C., Cohen, S. J. (1996). *Smoking Cessation. Clinical Practice Guideline No. 18*. Rockville, MD: U. S. Department of Health and Human Services, Public Health Service, Agency for Health Care Policy and Research. AHCPR Publication No. 96-0692.

Fiore, M. C., Jorenby, D. E., Baker, T. B., & Kenford, S. L. (1992). Tobacco dependence and the nicotine patch. *The Journal of the American Medical Association, 268*, 2687-2694.

Fiore, M. C., Smith, S. S., Jorneby, D. E., & Baker, T. B. (1994). The effectiveness of the nicotine patch for smoking cessation. A meta-analysis. *The Journal of the American Medical Association, 271*, 1940-1947.

George, H. Gallup International Institute. (1992). *Teen-age attitudes and behavior concerning tobacco: Report of the findings.* Princeton, NJ: George H. Gallup International Institute.

Gilman, A. G., Goodman, L. S., Rall, T. W., & Murad, F. (1985). *Goodman and Gilman's, The pharmacological basis of therapeutics* (7th Ed.). New York: Macmillan.

Glynn, T. J., Greenwald, P., Mills, S. M., & Manley, M. W. (1993). Youth tobacco use in the United States–problems, progress, goals, and potential solutions. *Preventive Medicine, 22*, 568-575.

Glynn, T., Anderson, J., & Schwartz, L. (1991). Tobacco-use reduction among high-risk youth: Recommendations of a National Cancer Institute Expert Advisory Panel. *Preventive Medicine, 20*, 279-291.

Guyer, B., Strobino, D. M., Ventura, S. J., & Singh, G. K. (1995). Annual summary of vital statistics–1994. *Pediatrics, 96*, 1029-1039.

Hays, J. T., Croghan, I. T., Offord, K. P., Hurt, R. D., Schroeder, D. R., Wolter, T. D., Nides, M. A., & Davidson, M. (1999). Over-the-counter nicotine patch therapy for smoking cessation: Results from randomized, double-blind, placebo-controlled and open label trials. *American Journal of Public Health, 89*, 1701-1709.

Henningfield, J. E., Clayton, R., & Pollin, W. (1990). Involvement of tobacco in alcoholism and illicit drug use. *British Journal of Addiction, 85*, 279-292.

Henningfield, J. E., & Keenan, R. M. (1993). Nicotine delivery kinetics and abuse liability. *Journal of Consulting and Clinical Psychology, 61*, 743-750.

Henningfield, J. E., Stapleton, J. M., Benowitz, N. L., Grayson, R. F., & London, E. D. (1993). Higher levels of nicotine in arterial than in venous blood after cigarette smoking. *Drug and Alcohol Dependence, 33*, 23-29.

Hjalmarson, A., Franzon, M., Westin, A., & Wiklund, O. (1994). Effect of nicotine nasal spray on smoking cessation. *Archives of Internal Medicine, 154*, 2567-2572.

Hollis, J.R., Vogt, T.M., Stevens, V., Biglan, A., Severson, H., & Lichtenstein, E. (1994). The Tobacco Reduction and Cancer Control (TRACC) Program: Team approaches to counseling in medical and dental settings. In: National Cancer Institute, *Tobacco and the Clinician: Interventions for Medical and Dental Practice. Smoking and Tobacco Control Monograph No. 5*. NIH Pub. No. 94-3693. USDHHS, 143-185.

Hughes, J. R. (1991). Long-term use of nicotine replacement therapy. In: *New developments in nicotine delivery systems*. Edited by Henningfield, J. E., & Stitzer, M. L. New York: Carlton, 64-71.

Hughes, J. R. (1993a). Pharmacotherapy for smoking cessation: Unvalidated assumptions, anomalies, and suggestions for future research. *Journal of Consulting and Clinical Psychology, 61*, 751-760.

Hughes, J. R. (1993b). Risk-benefit assessment of nicotine preparations in smoking cessation. *Drug Safety, 8*, 49-56.

Hughes, J. R. (1996). Treatment of nicotine dependence. In: *Pharmacological aspects of drug dependence: Toward an integrative neurobehavioral approach: Handbook of experimental psychology series, Vol. 11*. Edited by Schuster, D. R., Gust, S. W., Kuhar, M. J. New York: Springer-Verlag, 599-618.

Hughes, J. R., & Glaser, M. (1993). Transdermal nicotine for smoking cessation. *Health Values, 17*, 25-31.

Hughes, J. R., & Hatsukami, D, K. (1992). The nicotine withdrawal syndrome: A brief review and update. *International Journal of Smoking Cessation, 1*, 21-26.

Hughes, J. R., Higgins, S. T., & Hatsukami, D. (1990). Effects of abstinence from tobacco: A critical review. In: *Research advances in alcohol and drug problems, Vol. 10.* Edited by Kozlowski, L. T., Annis, H. M., Cappell, H. D., Glaser, F. B., Goodstadt, M. S., Israel, Y., Kalant, H., Sellers, E. M., Vingilis, E. R. New York: Plenum, 317-398.

Hurt, R. D., Dale, L. C., Croghan, G. A., Croghan, I. T., Gomez-Dahl, L. C., & Offord, K. P. (1998). Nicotine nasal spray for smoking cessation: Pattern of use, side effects, relief of withdrawal symptoms, and cotinine levels. *Mayo Clinic Proceedings, 73*, 118-125.

Hurt, R. D., Lauger, G. G., Offord, K. P., Kottke, T. E., & Dale, L. C. (1990). Nicotine replacement therapy with use of a transdermal nicotine patch. A randomized double-blind placebo-controlled trial. *Mayo Clinic Proceedings, 65*, 1529-1537.

Kandel, D., Chen, K., Warner, L. A., Kessler, R. C., & Grant, B. (1997). Prevalence and demographic correlates of symptoms of last year dependence on alcohol, nicotine, marijuana and cocaine in the U. S. population. *Drug and Alcohol Dependence, 44*, 11-29.

Kessler, D. (1995). Nicotine addiction in young people. *New England Journal of Medicine, 333*, 186-189.

Kornitzer, M., Boutsen, M., Dramaix, M., Thijs, J., & Gustavsson, G. (1995). Combined use of nicotine patch and gum in smoking cessation: A placebo-controlled clinical trial. *Preventive Medicine, 24*, 41-17.

Kottke, T., Solberg, L., Brekke, M., Conn, S. A., Maxwell, P., Brekke, M. J. (1992). A controlled trial to integrate smoking cessation advice into primary care practice: Doctors helping smokers, Round III. *Journal of Family Practice, 34*, 701-708.

Levenberg, P., & Elsterm, A. (1995). *Guidelines for Adolescent Preventive Services (GAPS),* American Medical Association Department of Adolescent Health. Chicago.

Lunell, E., Molander, L., & Leischow, S. (1995). Effect of nicotine vapour inhalation on the relief of tobacco withdrawal symptoms. *European Journal of Clinical Pharmacology, 48*, 235-240.

McGinnis, J. M., & Foerge, W. H. (1993). Actual causes of death in the United States. *Journal of the American Medical Association, 270*, 2207.

McNabb, M. E., Ebert, R. V., McCusker, K. (1982). Plasma nicotine levels produced by chewing nicotine gum. *Journal of the American Medical Association, 248*, 865-868.

McNeill, A. D., West, R. J., Jarvis, M., Jackson, P., & Bryant, A. (1986). Cigarette withdrawal symptoms in adolescent smokers. *Psychopharmacology, 90*, 533-536.

Mitchell, A. (1997). Nicotine replacement therapy on the NHS: Success rates of different smoking cessation treatments need to be compared. *British Medical Journal, 315*, 1381.

Montalto, N. J., & Garrett, S. D. (1998). Utilization of nicotine nasal spray in smoking cessation. *Journal of the American Osteopathic Association, 98*, 160-164.

Moss, A. J., Allen, K. F., & Giovino, G. A. (1992). Recent trends in adolescent smoking, smoking-uptake correlates, and expectations about the future. *Advance data from vital and health statistics. No. 221.* Hyattsville, MD: National Center for Health Statistics. DHHS Publication No. (PHS) 93-1250.

Myers, M. G., & Brown, S. A. (1994). Smoking and health in substance abusing adolescents: A two-year follow-up. *Pediatrics, 93*, 561-566.

McNeil Pharmaceuticals (Nicotrol®). (1996). Nicotine nasal spray prescribing information. McNeil Pharmaceuticals, Fort Washington, Pennsylvania.

McNeil Pharmaceuticals (Nicotrol®). (1997). Nicotine inhaler prescribing information. McNeil Pharmaceuticals, Fort Washington, Pennsylvania.

Oncken, C. A., Hardardottir, H., Hatsukami, D. K., Lupo, V. R., Rodis, J. F., & Smeltzer, J. S. (1997). Effects of transdermal nicotine or smoking on nicotine concentrations and maternal-fetal hemodynamics. *Obstetrics and Gynecology, 90*, 569-574.

Pallonen, U.E., Velicer, W.F., Prochaska, J.O., Rossi, J.S., Bellis, J.M., Tsoh, J.Y., Migneault, J.P., Smith, N.F., & Prokhorov, A.V. (1998). Computer-based cessation interventions in adolescents; Description, feasibility, and six-month follow-up findings. *Substance Use and Misuse, 33*, 1-31.

Palmer, K. H., & Faulds, D. (1992). Transdermal nicotine: A review of its pharmacodynamic and pharmacokinetic properties and therapeutic use as an aid to smoking cessation. *Drugs, 44*, 498-529.

Patten, C. A., & Martin, J. E. (1996). Does nicotine withdrawal affect smoking cessation? Clinical and theoretical issues. *Annals of Behavioral Medicine, 18*, 190-200.

Pederson, L. L., Koval, J. J. & O'Connor, K. (1997). Are psychosocial factors related to smoking in grade-6 students? *Addictive Behaviors, 22*, 169-181.

Pierce, J., Farkas, A., & Evans, N. (1993). *Tobacco use in California 1992: a focus on preventing uptake in adolescents*. Sacramento: California Department of Human Services.

Pirie, P. L., Murray, D. M., & Luepker, R. V. (1988). Smoking prevalence in a cohort of adolescents, including absentees, dropouts, and transfers. *American Journal of Public Health, 78*, 176-178.

Prokhorov, A. V., Pallonen, U. E., Fava, J. L., Ding, L., & Niaura, R. (1996). Measuring nicotine dependence among high-risk adolescent smokers. *Addictive Behaviors, 21*, 117-127.

Resnick, M. D., Bearman, P. S., Blum, R. W., Bauman, K. E., Harris, K. M., Jones, J., Tabor, J., Beuhring, T., Sieving, R., Shew, M., Ireland, M., Bearinger, L. H., & Udry, J. R. (1997). Protecting adolescents from harm: Findings from the National Longitudinal Study on Adolescent Health. *Journal of the American Medical Association, 278*, 823-832.

Rojas, N. L., Killen, J. D., Haydel, K. F., & Robinson, T. N. (1998). Nicotine dependence among adolescent smokers. *Archives of Pediatric and Adolescent Medicine, 152*, 151-156.

Rose, J. S., Chassin, L., Presson, C. C., & Sherman, S. J. (1996). Prospective predictors of quit attempts and smoking cessation in young adults. *Health Psychology, 15*, 261-268.

Rose, J. S., & Corrigall, W. A. (1997). Nicotine self-administration in animals and humans: Similarities and differences. *Psychopharmacology, 130*, 28-40.

Sarason, I. G., Mankowski, E. S., Peterson, A. V., & Dinh, K. T. (1992). Adolescent's reasons for Smoking. *Journal of School Health, 62*, 185-190.

Sargent, J. D., Mott, L. A., & Stevens, M. (1998). Predictors of smoking cessation in adolescents. *Archives of Pediatric and Adolescent Medicine, 152,* 388-393.

Schneider, N. G., Olmstead, R., Mody, F. V., Doan, K., Franzon, M., Jarvik, M. E., Steinberg, C. (1995). Efficacy of a nicotine nasal spray in smoking cessation–A placebo-controlled double-blind trial. *Addiction, 90,* 1671-1682.

Scholl, T. O., Salmon, R. W., & Miller, L. K. (1986). Smoking and adolescent pregnancy outcome. *Journal of Adolescent Health Care, 7,* 390-394.

Slade, J. (1993). Adolescent nicotine use and dependence. *Adolescent Medicine: State of the Art Reviews, 4,* 305-320.

Smith, T. A., House, R. F., Jr., Croghan, I. T., Gauvin, T. R., Colligan, R. C., Offord, K. P., Gomez-Dahl, L. C., & Hurt, R. D. (1996). Nicotine patch therapy in adolescent smokers. *Pediatrics, 98,* 659-667.

Stanton, W. R., Lowe, J. B., & Silva, P. A. (1995). Antecedents of vulnerability and resilience to smoking among adolescents. *Journal of Adolescent Health, 16,* 71-77.

Stone, S.L., & Kristeller, J.L. (1992). Attitudes of adolescents toward smoking cessation. *American Journal of Preventive Medicine, 8,* 185-190.

Sussman, S. (1997, August). Youth smoking cessation trials: Lessons learned. CDC Youth Tobacco Use Cessation Meeting. Atlanta, Georgia.

Sussman, S., Dent, C. W., Severson, H. H., Burton, D., & Flay, B. R. (1998). Self-initiated quitting among adolescent smokers. *Preventive Medicine, 27,* A19-A28.

Sussman, S., Lichtman, K., Ritt, A., & Pallonen, U. (1998a). Effects of thirty-four adolescent tobacco use and prevention trials on regular users of tobacco products. *Substance Use and Misuse, 34,* 1469-1503.

Sutherland, G., Russell, M. A. H., Stapleton, J., Feyerabend, C., & Ferno, O. (1992b). Nasal nicotine spray: A rapid nicotine delivery system. *Psychopharmacology, 108,* 512-518.

Sutherland, G., Stapleton, J. A., Russell, M. A. H., Jarvis, M. J., Hajek, P., Belcher, M., Feyerabend, C. (1992a). Randomized controlled trial of nasal nicotine spray in smoking cessation. *Lancet, 340,* 324-329.

Tonnesen, P., Nørregaard, J., Mikkelsen, K., Jorgensen, S., & Nilsson, F. (1993). A double-blind trial of a nicotine inhaler for smoking cessation. *Journal of the American Medical Association, 269,* 1268-1271.

Tonnesen, P., Nørregaard, J., Simonsen, K., & Sawe, U. (1991). A double-blind trial of a 16-hour transdermal nicotine patch in smoking cessation. *New England Journal of Medicine, 325,* 311-315.

U. S. Department of Health and Human Services. (1984). *The health consequences of smoking: Chronic obstructive lung disease. A report of the Surgeon General.* Washington, D.C., US DHHS, Public Health Service. DHHS Publication No. (CDC) 84-50205.

U. S. Department of Health and Human Services. (1987). *Drug abuse and drug abuse research, triennial report to Congress from the Secretary, Department of Health and Human Services.*

U. S. Department of Health and Human Services, National Institute on Drug Abuse, DHHS Publication No. (ADM) 87-1486. Washington, DC: U. S. Government Printing Office.

U. S. Department of Health and Human Services. (1988). *The health consequences of smoking: Nicotine addiction. A report of the U. S. Surgeon General.* DHHS Publication No. (CDC) 88-8406. Washington, DC: U. S. Government Printing Office.

U. S. Department of Health and Human Services. (1990). *The health benefits of smoking cessation. A report of the Surgeon General, 1990.* DHHS Publication No. (CDC) 90-8416. Rockville, MD: Public Health Service, Center for Disease Control, Office on Smoking and Health.

U. S. Department of Health and Human Services. (1994). Preventing tobacco use among young people: A report of the Surgeon General. *U.S. Public Health Service.* Centers for Disease Control and Prevention. National Center for Chronic Disease Prevention and Health Promotion, Office on Smoking and Health.

Wills, T. A., McNamara, G., Vaccaro, D., & Hirky, A.E. (1996). Escalated substance use: A longitudinal grouping from early to middle adolescence. *Journal of Abnormal Psychology, 105*, 16-180.

Wright, L. N., Thorp, J. M., Jr., Kuller, J. A., Shrewsbury, R. P., Ananth, C., & Hartmann, K. (1997). Transdermal nicotine replacement in pregnancy: Maternal pharmacokinetics and fetal effects. *American Journal of Obstetrics and Gynecology, 176,* 1090-1094,

A Smoking Intervention
for Substance Abusing Adolescents:
Outcomes, Predictors of Cessation Attempts,
and Post-Treatment Substance Use

Mark G. Myers
Sandra A. Brown
John F. Kelly

SUMMARY. Tobacco use is prevalent among youth with alcohol and other drug problems, yet this issue has been afforded limited research or clinical attention. The present study reports on findings for a cigarette smoking intervention for youth treated for substance abuse. Thirty-five adolescents, ages 13 to 18 (40% female), completed a cigarette-focused intervention and were followed-up at three months post-treatment. Six of the adolescents were abstinent from smoking at follow-up, while 17 had attempted cessation during the post-treatment period. Of baseline predictors examined, duration of smoking and intentions to quit pre-

Mark G. Myers, PhD, is affiliated with the Department of Psychiatry, University of California, San Diego and Psychology Service, Veterans Affairs San Diego Healthcare System. Sandra A. Brown, PhD, is affiliated with Departments of Psychiatry and Psychology, University of California, San Diego and Psychology Service, Veterans Affairs San Diego Healthcare System. John F. Kelly is affiliated with U.C. San Diego/San Diego State University Joint Doctoral Program.

Address correspondence to Mark Myers, PhD, Psychology 116B, V.A. Medical Center, 3350 La Jolla Village Dr., San Diego, CA 92161 (E-mail: mgmyers@ ucsd.edu).

This research was supported by a grant from the National Institute on Alcohol Abuse and Alcoholism (AA-11155).

[Haworth co-indexing entry note]: "A Smoking Intervention for Substance Abusing Adolescents: Outcomes, Predictors of Cessation Attempts, and Post-Treatment Substance Use." Myers, Mark G., Sandra Brown, and John F. Kelly. Co-published simultaneously in *Journal of Child & Adolescent Substance Abuse* (The Haworth Press, Inc.) Vol. 9, No. 4, 2000, pp. 77-91; and: *Nicotine Addiction Among Adolescents* (ed: Eric F. Wagner) The Haworth Press, Inc., 2000, pp. 77-91. Single or multiple copies of this article are available for a fee from The Haworth Document Delivery Service [1-800-342-9678, 9:00 a.m. - 5:00 p.m. (EST). E-mail address: getinfo@haworthpressinc.com].

77

dicted cessation attempts. Smoking cessation efforts had no negative impact on substance use outcomes. Findings were interpreted to provide support for the feasibility and utility of tobacco intervention in the context of adolescent substance abuse treatment. *[Article copies available for a fee from The Haworth Document Delivery Service: 1-800-342-9678. E-mail address: <getinfo@haworthpressinc.com> Website: <http://www.haworthpressinc. com>]*

KEYWORDS. Adolescence, smoking cessation, substance abuse, nicotine dependence

The issue of tobacco use and nicotine dependence among alcohol and other drug abusers has received increasing attention over the past decade. Concern regarding this issue stems from consistent findings that approximately 90% of adults treated for alcohol and other drug problems are cigarette smokers (e.g., Bien & Burge, 1990). Furthermore, a recent study found that tobacco-related diseases were the leading cause of death among a sample of adults treated for alcoholism (Hurt et al., 1996). Although several studies have addressed the problem of nicotine dependence among adult substance abusers (Hughes, 1993; Kalman, 1998), this issue has been afforded little research and clinical attention among adolescents treated for substance abuse.

Available research on tobacco use among adolescents treated for substance abuse demonstrates that cigarette smoking is prevalent and persists for years following treatment. An early study of smoking among 132 substance abusing adolescents found 113 (86%) reported current cigarette smoking, with 75% smoking daily and 65% smoking ten or more cigarettes daily (Myers & Brown, 1990). The smokers reported a mean daily consumption of 15.5 cigarettes, and there were no gender differences in smoking prevalence. This study provided initial evidence that alcohol and other drug abusing youth show levels of cigarette involvement comparable to adult alcoholics. A second study followed this same sample for two years after completing alcohol and drug abuse treatment (Myers & Brown, 1994). We found continued high rates of cigarette use, but an overall decrease in prevalence and percent of daily smokers. Examination of cigarette smoking in relation to post-treatment outcome found that smoking persisted at equally high rates regardless of alcohol and other drug use outcomes. We also found that adolescents reporting post-treatment respiratory problems smoked more, and heavier smokers at the time of treatment were more likely to report respiratory problems at follow-up than lighter smokers. A subsequent investigation reported on adolescent smoking four years after treatment (Myers & Brown, 1997). Eighty percent of youth smoking at the time of treatment were still smoking four years later. Age of initial cigarette use and extent of smoking at the time of treatment significantly predicted late adolescent/early adult smoking for male but not female participants. Those no longer smoking at the four-year time-point reported less alcohol and drug involvement than those who were still smoking.

We recently have reported preliminary findings describing cigarette smoking and cessation efforts for a separate sample of 49 substance abusing adolescents in treatment (60% female, 84% white) (Myers, Kelly, & Lennox, 1997). Forty (81%) of these adolescents were current smokers, whose mean consumption was 14.6 cigarettes per day and mean Fagerstrom Tolerance Questionnaire score was 3.6 (suggesting low tobacco dependence). Sixty-three percent of the smokers had attempted to quit within the previous year, with health concerns cited as the primary motive for prior quit attempts. Overall, participants were moderately motivated to quit smoking. These data replicated earlier findings of high smoking rates and added information regarding nicotine dependence and cessation efforts among substance abusing adolescents. Importantly, these findings suggested that many youth treated for substance abuse had previously attempted smoking cessation and may be motivated to participate in a tobacco-focused intervention. In sum, our studies of cigarette smoking among youth treated for alcohol and other drug abuse documented high rates of smoking, smoking-related health consequences during adolescence, substantial persistence of smoking into early adulthood, and interest in smoking cessation. The high prevalence and persistence of smoking among substance abusing adolescents and associated health problems identifies this group as a particularly important target for smoking treatment.

In response to the need for smoking treatment for substance abusing adolescents, we undertook a project to develop and implement a cigarette smoking intervention designed specifically for this population. The primary goals of this project were to develop a treatment manual and demonstrate the feasibility of implementing smoking intervention in the context of treatment for alcohol and other drug abuse. Limited guidance was available for selecting intervention content since the few published studies to date on adolescent smoking cessation treatment reported little or no success in achieving significant rates of cessation (e.g., Institute of Medicine, 1994; Sussman et al., in press; USDHHS, 1994). As such, components included in the intervention were derived from available research regarding correlates of adolescent smoking cessation and persistence, developmental considerations, effective strategies for adult smoking cessation, and substance abuser specific factors (see Myers, Brown, & Kelly, in press, for a detailed description of intervention content).

A review of naturalistic studies on the progression and persistence of youth cigarette smoking identified several important predictors of smoking cessation efforts: extent of smoking history (Ary & Biglan, 1988; Ershler et al., 1989;

Hansen, 1983; Sargent, Mott, & Stevens, 1998; Sussman et al., 1998a), peer smoking (Ary & Biglan, 1988; Chassin, Presson, & Sherman, 1984; Ershler et al., 1989), family influences (Chassin, Presson, Sherman, & Edwards 1991; Sussman et al., 1998a), and intentions to smoke (Ary & Biglan, 1988; Sargent, Mott, & Stevens, 1998; Sussman et al., 1998a). While not exhaustive, these domains represented factors that could be addressed and modified in the context of treatment. The intervention was tailored for substance abusing youth by addressing similarities and differences between cigarette use and alcohol and other drug abuse. Each application of the intervention addressed these primary domains, and successive versions were modified based on previous experience and participant feedback. Thus, the format of the intervention (e.g., number of group meetings, sequence of topics, etc.) varied over time and cohorts. The treatment was designed for all adolescent smokers in treatment for substance abuse, regardless of motivation for cessation. As such, the content was tailored to be appropriate for adolescents with varying levels of readiness to engage in behavior change (e.g., smoking cessation was presented as one of several possible treatment goals). Thus, the primary objectives of treatment were to encourage initial changes in cigarette use, motivate cessation attempts, and provide adolescents with skills and strategies for successful behavior change. A preliminary examination of 1 month post-treatment data from this developmental project provided support for treatment feasibility and suggested the intervention produced decreases in cigarette smoking and motivated cessation attempts (Myers, Brown, Kelly, & Tapert, 1997).

A long-standing concern in addiction treatment is the potential for quitting smoking to interfere with the achievement and maintenance of abstinence from alcohol and other drugs (Bobo & Gilchrist, 1983; Bobo et al., 1987). However, available studies examining smoking cessation among adult drug and alcohol abusers do not support the notion of increased risk for relapse (Hughes, 1993; Martin et al., 1997; Sees & Clark, 1993). A recent review of existing studies on this topic concluded that voluntary smoking cessation at the time of alcohol and other drug treatment does not appear to have any adverse effects on substance use outcomes (Kalman, 1998). To date, no information is available regarding the influence of smoking cessation efforts on adolescent substance abuse treatment outcomes. Therefore, an additional aim of the present study was to provide initial data as to the potential effects of smoking cessation on alcohol and other drug use.

The current study reports on outcomes three months following smoking treatment, examines baseline predictors of cessation attempts during the post-treatment period, and explores the relation between smoking cessation attempts and substance use relapse among adolescents treated for substance abuse and dependency. We use smoking cessation attempts (vs. smoking cessation) as our primary outcome variable because of sample size limitations and since this variable represented a major goal of the treatment. Predictors examined in relation to smoking cessation attempts included: nicotine dependence; peer smoking influences; parental smoking; and intentions to quit. Because of conflicting findings regarding the effect of gender on adolescent cessation (Sussman et al., 1998a), we also explored the role of gender in predicting smoking cessation attempts. We hypothesized that less tobacco use involvement, fewer smoking peers, less parental smoking, and greater intention to quit smoking would correspond positively with attempted cessation following treatment completion. Since studies of smoking cessation among adult substance abusers suggest no detrimental influence on alcohol and other drug outcomes, we anticipated that adolescents who attempted smoking cessation would have similar substance use outcomes to those who did not attempt cessation.

METHODS

Participants

Participating adolescents were recruited from two outpatient substance abuse treatment programs and a community-based recovery program in metropolitan San Diego, California. Informed consent was obtained separately from adolescent participants and a parent/legal guardian.

Participating adolescents met *Diagnostic and Statistical Manual for Psychiatric Disorders* IV (DSM-IV; American Psychiatric Association, 1994) criteria for lifetime abuse of alcohol or an illicit drug and smoked cigarettes at least once a week. A parent or legal guardian provided corroborative historical data and current substance involvement information.

Thirty-five adolescents participated in the treatment development project over a two year period, of whom 31 (89%) completed one-month and 28 (80%) completed three-month post-treatment interviews. The number of sessions offered to each group varied from 5 to 8, and all participants included in the present analyses attended at least 3 sessions. Participants varied in terms of length of alcohol and drug abstinence prior to attending the smoking intervention, ranging from a few weeks prior to one year. Participants were on average 16.2 years of age (range 13-18), and the sample was 40% female and 71% white.

Procedure

Participating adolescents and their parents were assessed separately at the start of smoking groups and again one and three months following intervention completion. The intake interview was conducted in person and assessed demographic information, a variety of smoking-related variables, and current and lifetime cigarette, alcohol, and other drug use. The one- and three-month follow-up interviews assessed smoking cessation efforts and cigarette, alcohol, and other drug use during the preceding interval (i.e., 30 or 60 days, respectively). The one-month follow-up interviews were conducted by telephone, and the three-month assessments were done in person. Parent reports were utilized to corroborate adolescent self-reports of cigarette, alcohol and other drug use. At three months, adolescent smoking status was verified using expired breath carbon monoxide (CO) measures.

Intervention

Intervention delivery varied during the course of treatment development; the initial two cohorts met for eight sessions, and subsequent cohorts met for five to six sessions. Our current standard version of the intervention is six sessions, and this is what most of the participants received.

Despite variation in number of sessions, the core content of the intervention was delivered in similar fashion to all participants across cohorts. Motivational strategies employed included examining personal experiences with smoking, with an emphasis on positive and negative consequences, providing information relevant to adolescent smokers, and allowing participants to select goals for behavior change during the course of treatment. Similarly all cohorts were provided with behavioral strategies for reducing quantity and frequency of cigarette use and skills for coping with urges to smoke and relapse prevention. Finally, social aspects of adolescent smoking were discussed in all cohorts, with an emphasis on obtaining support for smoking cessation and assertive skills for refusing offers of cigarettes.

Measures

Intake Questionnaire: This assessment is an abbreviated version of the Structured Clinical Interview (SCI) developed by Sandra Brown for studying adolescent substance abusers (Brown, Vik, & Creamer, 1989). This intake interview assesses demographics (age, socioeconomic status, education, family characteristics, etc.), treatment history, and psychosocial functioning (e.g., academics, extracurricular activities, social functioning).

Teen Smoking Questionnaire (TSQ): This instrument is composed of items from various existing smoking-related measures, and assesses lifetime smoking history (age of onset, rate of heaviest smoking, past [lifetime] and recent [past three months] attempts at smoking cessation), and motivation and self-efficacy for quitting smoking. It also incorporates the most commonly used measure of nicotine dependence, the Fagerstrom Tolerance Questionnaire

(FTQ) (Fagerstrom & Schneider, 1989), from which Fagerstrom Test for Nicotine Dependence (FTND) (Heatherton, et al., 1991) scores were derived for the current study. In addition, the questionnaire includes items derived from the Health Behavior Questionnaire–high school form (Donovan & Jessor, 1992) assessing peer and parental smoking and attitudes toward smoking. The TSQ was repeated at the three-month interview, omitting historical use items.

Time-Line Followback (TLFB) (Sobell & Sobell, 1992): The TLFB was employed to gather information regarding cigarette use quantity and frequency, and alcohol and other drug use frequency during the 30 days preceding the intake and one-month interview, and for 60 days preceding the three-month interview. Results from the TLFB were used to establish point-prevalence for smoking cessation (no smoking in the previous week). The TLFB has been shown to have good reliability and validity with adult smokers (R. Brown et al., 1998), and initial reports demonstrate the utility of the TLFB with adolescent alcohol and other drug abusers (Turner, Dakof, & Liddle, 1996; Waldron, 1996).

RESULTS

Post-Treatment Smoking

Data from the one- and three-month follow-up interviews were combined to reflect the full post-treatment interval. At the three-month time-point six participants (21% of participants at three-months) reported abstinence from smoking for at least the prior seven days. Average number of days abstinent during the follow-up interval for those who had quit was 65.7 out of 90 (*sd* = 19.1; range = 37 to 90 days). Length of continuous days without smoking during the follow-up interval averaged 55.2 (*sd* = 30.7, range = 19 to 90 days).

Two of the participants had quit smoking during the smoking intervention and maintained continuous abstinence, and therefore were not included in analyses predicting post-treatment cessation attempts. Seventeen of the remaining 28 (61%) had attempted cessation at least once during the follow-up interval. Among these participants, eleven tried quitting once, one tried twice, four tried three times, and one tried six times. Those who attempted cessation at least once reported an average of 27.9 smoke-free days (*sd* = 27.6; range = 1 to 83).

Predictors of Cessation Attempts

Predictors of smoking cessation efforts were examined by comparing those who made at least one attempt following treatment (n = 16) with those who made no attempts (n = 12). Table 1 displays overall and group proportions or means and standard deviations for each of the baseline predictors. Of the variables examined, only two baseline predictors approached significance: likelihood of not smoking in the future $(F(1, 27) = 3.3, p = .08)$ and years since onset of weekly smoking $(F(1, 27) = 4.1, p = .05)$. Adolescents who attempted cessation following treatment tended to to anticipate a higher likelihood of not smoking in the future and have a longer smoking history.

Smoking Cessation Attempts in Relation to Substance Use Relapse

The relationship between smoking cessation attempts and post-treatment substance use was examined in two ways. Those who attempted cessation were compared to those with no cessation attempts on the total number of post-treatment days abstinent (using ANOVA), and on whether a relapse to alcohol or other drugs had occurred (using χ^2). No differences were found between the groups on average number of days abstinent from alcohol and drugs (see Table 2). Of the 28 participants interviewed at the three-month time-point, only six reported any use of alcohol and/or drugs. While 33% (4/12) of those who did not attempt cessation reported a relapse, only 13% (2/16) of those attempting smoking cessation relapsed. However, this difference was not statistically significant.

TABLE 1. Comparison of Baseline Predictors Between Adolescents Who Attempted Smoking Cessation Following Treatment and Those Who Did Not Attempt Cessation

Baseline Predictor Variable	Attempted cessation	Did not attempt cessation	Total (full sample)
	(n = 16)	(n = 12)	
FTND score (M(sd)) Range: 0-8	3.2 (2.5)	2.9 (3.1)	3.4 (2.7)
†Years since weekly smoking onset (M(sd)) Range:1-7	3.7 (1.8)	2.5 (1.4)	3.2 (1.7)
Proportion of friends smoking (M(sd)) Range: 2-10	7.8 (2.4)	7.3 (2.6)	7.55 (2.46)
Proportion with parents who smoked	29%	33%	31%
†Likelihood of being a non-smoker (M(sd)) Range: 1-10	5.7 (2.6)	3.6 (3.5)	4.89 (3.08)
Proportion female	41%	42%	41%

Note: † $p < .10$

TABLE 2. Comparison of Substance Abuse Outcomes Between Adolescents Who Attempted Smoking Cessation and Those Who Did Not Attempt Cessation Following Smoking Treatment

Substance Use Variable	Attempted cessation (n = 16)	Did not attempt cessation (n = 12)
Proportion relapsed	13%	33%
Average number of days abstinent (M(sd))	89.5 (1.5)	83.3 (21.3)

DISCUSSION

The present study reports on results from a project concerning the development of a cigarette smoking intervention for treated substance abusing youth. Outcomes assessed during the three months following treatment reveal that over half of the participants met the goal of attempted smoking cessation, and six were abstinent from nicotine at follow-up. Of baseline predictors, only length of smoking history and intentions to quit distinguished between adolescents who did and did not attempt cessation. No differences in alcohol and other drug use outcomes were observed between adolescents who attempted smoking cessation and those who did not.

Results from this developmental project support the feasibility of our treatment for motivating smoking cessation attempts among substance abusing youth. Although only two participants had stopped smoking by the end of treatment, six adolescents were abstinent at the three-month follow-up. The point-prevalence criterion used in this study is less stringent than that of continuous abstinence; however, the nicotine abstinent teens reported an average of over 60 smoke-free days. Similarly, while few participants attempted cessation during the course of treatment, over half attempted cessation during the three-month post-treatment period. Those attempting cessation reported an average of almost 30 smoke-free days, and several engaged in multiple smoking cessation attempts. Thus, adolescents in the present study made substantial efforts at changing their smoking behavior following the intervention. It is noteworthy that smoking outcomes improved from the end of treatment to three months post-treatment. In the absence of a control group, conclusions cannot be drawn regarding the efficacy of this intervention. However, these data support the feasibility of intervening with cigarette use among adolescents treated for alcohol and other drug abuse, and indicate that the present intervention shows promise in effecting smoking cessation attempts.

Investigation of baseline predictors of smoking cessation attempts was limited by the small sample size and restricted range of predictor variables. The predictor domains examined by and large did not distinguish between adolescents who attempted cessation and those who did not.

Variations in the extent of smoking and nicotine dependence have consistently predicted adolescent smoking cessation in naturalistic studies, yet in the present study no differences emerged. One possible reason for this discrepant finding is that nicotine dependence is found to predict successful cessation but has not typically been examined in relation to cessation attempts. Thus, extent of dependence may influence sustained success at quitting rather than attempts at quitting. A trend emerged whereby those who attempted to quit smoking had a longer smoking history, a finding opposite to that predicted. A post-hoc analysis revealed a low correlation between smoking history and Fagerstrom scores ($r = .18$), suggesting that among adolescents' length of smoking history is not isomorphic with extent of nicotine dependence. It may be that smoking-related negative consequences and hassles accrue over time regardless of nicotine dependence. These accumulated consequences may serve to motivate cessation, and thereby increase the likelihood of cessation attempts.

Predictors reflecting peer and familial influences also failed to distinguish between those who did and did not attempt smoking cessation. The lack of group differences in proportion of smoking friends may reflect the very high rates of smoking among peers of substance abusing adolescents, which was estimated as over 70% of peers in the present sample. Prior studies on parental influences suggest that parental smoking decreases the likelihood of smoking cessation (e.g., Chassin, Presson, Sherman, & Edwards, 1991). In the present study, parental smoking did not appear to influence smoking cessation efforts. Given the power of social influences during adolescence, it is significant that these do not appear to dissuade smoking cessation attempts (in the present sample) for at least a portion of substance abusing adolescents. This is particularly noteworthy given the high prevalence of peer smoking for this group of youth.

The final predictor domain examined was that of intentions to quit, a motivational variable previously found to be associated with adolescent smoking cessation. In the present sample, those who attempted cessation tended to score higher on their rating of likelihood of being a non-smoker in a year. This finding is consistent with previous research and reinforces the role of motivation in behavior change efforts for substance abusing adolescents.

Although conflicting findings exist with regard to the influence of gender on cessation attempts and successful smoking cessation among adolescents and adults, several investigators have noted the importance of gender-specific considerations in the smoking cessation treatment (e.g., Royce et al., 1997;

see Wagner & Atkins, this publication). In the present sample, similar proportions of boys and girls attempted cessation. However, cessation attempts reflect only a single aspect of the cessation process. A recent study of adolescent quitting and temptations (Sussman et al., 1998b) found boys and girls similar on attitudes regarding cessation and reasons for quitting, yet differences emerged on smoking temptations. These findings were interpreted to suggest that functional aspects of smoking more salient to females may impede cessation efforts. Thus, more detailed investigations of the adolescent smoking cessation process are necessary to determine the need for gender-specific intervention components.

Several factors in the present study may have contributed to the limited prediction of smoking cessation attempts. Previous evidence for the predictor domains selected was drawn from naturalistic studies of smoking cessation. These studies differ from the present investigation in important ways. First, the present study was not naturalistic, but rather involved active treatment. Therefore, one possibility is that treatment served to moderate the effect of traditional predictors of outcome. For example, a focus on smoking-related social issues may have served to buffer the considerable pro-smoking peer influences experienced by youth in this sample. This speculation must be confirmed with findings from controlled studies of treatment outcome for the present intervention. Another difference from previous studies was our reliance on smoking cessation attempts as the primary measure of outcome. Evidence that more frequent cessation attempts are associated with adolescent smoking cessation (e.g., Green, 1979; US DHHS, 1982) suggests that similar factors may act in both cases. However, studies that distinguish predictors of cessation attempts from successful cessation efforts are needed to further inform the design of adolescent smoking cessation treatment.

Demonstrating that smoking cessation does not detrimentally influence abstinence from alcohol and other drugs is important for promoting tobacco interventions within addiction treatment settings. Findings from the present study suggest no negative effect on alcohol and drug abstinence from smoking cessation efforts by adolescents. Although not statistically significant, the proportion of alcohol and drug relapses was lower among those attempting smoking cessation compared with adolescents who did not attempt to quit smoking (13% versus 33%, respectively). Similarly, both smoking outcome groups were similar on number of days abstinent from alcohol and drugs. These data provide preliminary evidence that smoking cessation intervention in the context of adolescent addiction treatment poses no risk to substance use outcome.

Several limitations of the present study must be considered when interpreting the present data. Intervention delivery during this project varied across cohorts, and no control group was available. Thus, one cannot view the present results as evidence for intervention efficacy. The outcomes reported, in particular the high rates of smoking cessation efforts, are encouraging and deserve further investigation. The small sample size dictated limited data analysis and power for detecting differences. The differences that did emerge in the present study can serve to guide future research directions. Finally, the choice of predictors was based on a literature that focused on smoking cessation and persistence, rather than smoking cessation per se. However, identifying predictors of cessation attempts is valuable for treatment design, in particular when intervening with a population such as this that includes widely varying levels of initial motivation to change smoking behavior.

The present results demonstrate clearly that substance abusing adolescents can be engaged in efforts to change their cigarette smoking behaviors. This finding is particularly important given the lack of success encountered by most published adolescent smoking cessation studies to date. While it is premature to discuss specific treatment components that may produce behavior change, some strategic aspects of this intervention development study may contribute to the observed outcomes. In particular, the advantage of addressing tobacco use in the context of substance abuse treatment is that it targets a population in great need and overcomes recruitment difficulties common to adolescent smoking cessation efforts. By incorporating tobacco intervention as part of addiction treatment, all adolescent smokers in treatment for substance abuse will be educated regarding nicotine dependence and receive training in skills relevant to smoking cessation. Furthermore, addressing tobacco use in the context of substance abuse treatment provides a more consistent message regarding addiction and utilizes similar skills to promote and sustain behavior change. The finding that smoking cessation efforts do not detrimentally influence substance use outcomes supports further the value of making tobacco intervention standard practice when treating adolescent substance abuse.

REFERENCES

Ary, D.V., & Biglan, A. (1988). Longitudinal changes in adolescent smoking behavior: Onset and cessation. *Journal of Behavioral Medicine, 11*, 361-382.

Bien, T.H., & Burge, R. (1990). Smoking and drinking: A review of the literature. *International Journal of the Addictions, 25*, 1429-1451.

Bobo, J.K., & Gilchrist, L.D. (1983) Urging the alcoholic client to quit smoking cigarettes. *Addictive Behaviors. 8*, 297-305.

Bobo, J.K., Gilchrist, L.D., Schilling, R.F., Noach, B., & Schinke, S.P. (1987). Cigarette smoking cessation attempts by recovering alcoholics. *Addictive Behaviors, 13*, 209-215.

Brown, R.A., Burgess, E.S., Sales, S.D., Whitely, J.A., Evans, D.M., & Miller, I.W. (1998). Reliability and validity of a smoking time-line follow-back interview. *Psychology of Addictive Behaviors, 12,101*-112.

Brown, S.A., Vik, P.W., & Creamer, V.A. (1989). Characteristics of relapse following adolescent substance abuse treatment. *Addictive Behaviors, 14*, 291-300

Chassin, L., Presson, C.C., & Sherman, S.J. (1984). Cognitive and social influence factors in adolescent smoking cessation. *Addictive Behaviors, 9*, 383-390.

Chassin, L., Presson, C.C., Sherman, S.J. & Edwards, D.A. (1991). Four pathways to young-adult smoking status: adolescent social-psychological antecedents in a Midwestern community sample. *Health Psychology, 10*, 409-418.

Donovan, J.E., & Jessor,R. (1992). Health Behavior Questionnaire: High school form. *Institute of Behavioral Science.* University of Colorado.

Ershler, J., Leventhal, H., Fleming, R., & Glynn, K. (1989). The quitting experience for smokers in sixth through twelfth grades. *Addictive Behaviors, 14*, 365-378.

Fagerstrom, K., & Schneider, N.G. (1989). Measuring nicotine dependence: A review of the Fagerstrom Tolerance Questionnaire. *Journal of Behavioral Medicine, 12*, 159-182.

Heatherton, T.F., Kozlowski, L.T., Frecker, R.C., & Fagerstrom, K. (1991). The Fagerstom test for nicotine dependence: A revision of the Fagerstrom Tolerance Questionnaire. *British Journal of Addiction, 86*, 1119-1127.

Hughes, J.R. (1993). Treatment of smoking cessation in smokers with past alcohol/drug problems. *Journal of Substance Abuse Treatment, 10*, 181-187.

Hurt, R.D., Offord, K.P., Croghan, I.T., Gomez-Dahl, L., Kottke, T.E., Morse, R.M., & Melton, L.J. (1996). Mortality following inpatient addictions treatment: Role of tobacco use in a community-based cohort. *Journal of the American Medical Association, 275*, 1097-1103.

Institute of Medicine (1994). *Growing Up Tobacco Free.* Washington, DC: National Academy Press.

Johnston, L.D., O'Malley, P.M., Bachman, J.G. (1992). *Smoking, drinking, and illicit drug use among American secondary school students, college students, and young adults, 1975-1991: Volume I, secondary school students.* U.S. Department of Health and Human Service, Public Health Service, National Institutes of Health, National Institute on Drug Abuse. Bethesda, MD: NIH Publication No. 93-3480, 1992a.

Johnston, L.D., O'Malley, P.M., Bachman, J.G. (1993). *National Survey Results on Drug Use from The Monitoring the Future Study, 1975-1992: Volume I, secondary school students.* U.S. Department of Health and Human Service, Public Health Service, National Institutes of Health, National Institute on Drug Abuse. Bethesda, MD: NIH Publication No. 93-3957.

Kalman, D. (1998). Smoking cessation treatment for substance misusers in early recovery: A review of the literature and recommendations for practice. *Substance Use and Misuse, 33*, 2021-2047.

Martin, J.E., Calfas, K.J., Patten, C.A., Polarek, M., Hofstetter, C.R., Noto, J., & Beach, D. (1997). Prospective evaluation of three smoking interventions in 205 recovering alcoholics: One year results of Project SCRAP-Tobacco. *Journal of Consulting and Clinical Psychology, 65*, 190 194.

Myers, M.G., & Brown, S.A.(1990). Cigarette smoking and health among adolescent substance abusers. Paper presented at The Society of Behavioral Medicine Annual Meeting, Chicago, April 1990.

Myers, M.G. & Brown, S.A. (1994). Smoking and health in substance abusing adolescents: A two year follow-up. *Pediatrics, 93*, 561-566.

Myers, M.G., & Brown, S.A. (1997). Cigarette smoking four years following treatment for adolescent substance abuse. *Journal of Child and Adolescent Substance Abuse, 7,* 1-15.

Myers, M.G., Brown, S.A., & Kelly, J.F. (in press). A Cigarette Smoking Intervention for Substance Abusing Adolescents. Cognitive and Behavioral Practice.

Myers, M.G., Brown, S.A., Kelly, J.F., & Tapert, S.F. A cigarette smoking intervention for substance abusing adolescents: Preliminary findings. Fromme, K. (Symposium chair), Empirically based prevention and treatment for adolescent and young adult substance use. Symposium paper presented at the Association for Advancement of Behavior Therapy Annual Meeting, Miami Beach, FL November 1997.

Myers, M.G., Kelly, J., & Lennox, G.A. Nicotine dependence and motivation for smoking cessation among substance abusing adolescents. Poster presented at the Society of Behavioral Medicine Annual Meeting, San Francisco, CA, April 1997.

Nelson, D.E., Giovino, G.A., Shopland, D.R., Mowery, P.D., Mills, S.L., & Eriksen, M.P (1995). Trends in cigarette smoking among U.S. adolescents, 1974 through 1991. *American Journal of Public Health, 85,* 34-40.

Rosengren, A., Wilhelmsen, L., & Wedel H. (1988). Separate and combined effects of smoking and alcohol abuse in middle-aged men. *Acta Medica Scandinavia, 223,* 111-118.

Royce, J.M., Corbett, K., Sorensen, G., & Ockene, J. (1997). Gender, social pressure, and smoking cessations: The Community Intervention Trial for Smoking Cessation (COMMIT) at baseline. *Social Science and Medicine, 44,* 359-370.

Sargent, J.D., Mott, LA., & Stevens, M. (1998). Predictors of smoking cessation in adolescents. *Archives of Pediatrics and Adolescent Medicine, 152* (4), 388-393.

Sees, K.L., & Clark, H.W. (1993). When to begin smoking cessation in substance abusers. *Journal of Substance Abuse Treatment, 10,* 189-195.

Sobell, L.C., & Sobell, M.B. (1992). Time-line follow-back: A technique for assessing self reported alcohol consumption. In R.Z. Litten & J.P. Allen (Eds.), *Measuring Alcohol Consumption* (pp. 73-98). Totowa, NJ: Humana Press. New York, NY: Pergamon Press.

Sussman,S., Dent, C.W., Severson, H., Burton,D., & Flay, B.R. (1998a). Self-initiated quitting among adolescent smokers. *Preventive Medicine, 27,* A19-A28.

Sussman,S., Dent, C.W., Nezami, E., Stacy, A., Burton,D., & Flay, B.R. (1998b). Reasons for quitting and smoking temptation among adolescent smokers: Gender differences. *Substance Use and Misuse, 33,* 2705-2722.

Sussman, S., Lichtman, K., Ritt, A. & Pallonen, U. (in press). Effects of thirty four adolescent tobacco use cessation and prevention trials on regular users of tobacco products. *Substance Use and Misuse.*

Turner, R.M., Dakof, G., & Liddle, H. (1996). The structure and developmental trajectory of inner city adolescents' substance abusing behavior. In R.M. Turner (Chair) Assessment, structure and developmental trajectories of adolescent substance abuse. Proceedings for the 30th Association for Advancement of Behavior Therapy Annual Meeting. P.67.

U. S. Department of Health and Human Services (1985). *The health consequences of smoking: Cancer and chronic lung disease in the workplace: A report of the*

Surgeon General. Rockville, MD: Office on Smoking and Health, U.S. Public Health Service.

U. S. Department of Health and Human Services (1990). *The health benefits of smoking cessation: A report of the Surgeon General*. Rockville, MD: Office on Smoking and Health, U.S. Public Health Service.

U. S. Department of Health and Human Services (1994). *Preventing tobacco use among young people: A report of the Surgeon General*. Atlanta, GA: U.S. Department of Health and Human Services, Public Health Service, Centers for Disease Control and Prevention, National Center for Chronic Disease Prevention and Health Promotion, Office on Smoking.

U. S. Department of Health and Human Services (1995). *Monitoring the Future Study: Summary of findings through 1995*. Washington DC: U. S. Department of Health and Human Services.

U. S. Department of Health and Human Services (1996). Clinical Practice Guideline Number 18, *Smoking Cessation*. (AHCPR Publication No. 96-0692). Washington, DC: U.S. Government Printing Office.

Waldron, H.B. (1996). Developments in assessing adolescent alcohol use. In R.M. Turner (Chair) Assessment, structure and developmental trajectories of adolescent substance abuse. Proceedings for the 30th Association for Advancement of Behavior Therapy Annual Meeting. P.67.

Smoking Among Teenage Girls

Eric F. Wagner
Jana H. Atkins

SUMMARY. The current paper reviews the existing literature about smoking among teenage girls. We begin with a summary of recent epidemiological data concerning gender differences in the rates of various smoking behaviors among adolescents. We next focus on how gender may influence smoking initiation, maintenance, and cessation among adolescents. Specifically, we examine weight control motives, social influences, mood management motives, and image-related motives as particularly important factors in teenage girls' smoking. We then offer a brief review of some of the more popular adolescent smoking interventions. We conclude the paper with recommendations for ways in which the effectiveness of smoking prevention and intervention programs for girls may be improved. *[Article copies available for a fee from The Haworth Document Delivery Service: 1-800-342-9678. E-mail address: <getinfo@haworthpressinc.com> Website: <http://www.haworthpressinc.com>]*

KEYWORDS. Smoking, adolescence, females

The prevalence of cigarette smoking during adolescence is approximately equal across girls and boys. While eighth and tenth grade girls are slightly

Eric F. Wagner, PhD, is affiliated with College of Urban and Public Affairs, Florida International University. Jana H. Atkins, MS, is affiliated with Center for Psychological Studies, Nova Southeastern University.

Address correspondence to Eric F. Wagner, PhD, College of Urban and Public Affairs, Florida International University, North Campus, AC-1, Suite 200, North Miami, FL 33181-3600 (E-mail: wagnere@fiu.edu).

Preparation of this article was supported in part by National Institute on Alcohol Abuse and Alcoholism Grant AA10246.

[Haworth co-indexing entry note]: "Smoking Among Teenage Girls." Wagner, Eric F., and Jana H. Atkins. Co-published simultaneously in *Journal of Child & Adolescent Substance Abuse* (The Haworth Press, Inc.) Vol. 9, No. 4, 2000, pp. 93-110; and: *Nicotine Addiction Among Adolescents* (ed: Eric F. Wagner) The Haworth Press, Inc., 2000, pp. 93-110. Single or multiple copies of this article are available for a fee from The Haworth Document Delivery Service [1-800-342-9678, 9:00 a.m. - 5:00 p.m. (EST). E-mail address: getinfo@haworthpressinc.com].

more likely than same-aged boys to report past month smoking (19.8% vs. 18.0% in 8th grade; 29.1% vs. 26.2% in 10th grade), twelfth grade girls are slightly less likely to report past month smoking than same-aged boys (33.3% vs. 36.3%) (University of Michigan, 1998). However, equality between the genders in rates of smoking has not always been the case. Johnston, O'Malley, and Bachman (1998) reported that adolescent girls were less likely to smoke cigarettes than adolescent boys prior to the 1970s. Girls caught up to and passed boys in regard to smoking during the 1970s, and remained more likely to smoke than boys throughout the 1980s. In the early 1990s, girls' smoking dropped below boys' smoking, and from 1992 through 1998 both genders showed increases in smoking rates. Currently, over one-third of American students actively smoke by the time they leave high school, regardless of gender.

While the likelihood of smoking during adolescence is comparable across girls and boys, the likelihood of cessation attempts is not. In a recent study of teenage daily smokers, the Centers for Disease Control (1998) found females (77.6%) were more likely than males (68.7%) to have attempted to quit smoking during high school. There was no evidence that girls were any more successful than boys in their quit attempts, though it should be noted that female gender has been related to lower quit rates in some studies, but not in others (see Sussman, Dent, Severson, Burton, & Flay, 1998). Additionally, the influence of early quit attempts (i.e., during the teens) on long-term success in smoking cessation remains unknown. However, the fact that girls were more likely to attempt quitting suggests that they might be especially receptive to interventions in support of their cessation attempts. Furthermore, the expected duration of smoking differs by gender. Data from the National Health Interview Surveys indicate that the median cessation age for individuals who start smoking during adolescence is 33 years for males and 37 years for females (Pierce & Gilpin, 1996).

In sum, epidemiological research indicates that girls were less likely to smoke than boys prior to the 1970s, were more likely to smoke than boys during the late 1970s and 1980s, and are about as likely to smoke as boys currently. In addition, girls who smoke are more likely to try to quit smoking than boys, but do not appear to be any more successful in their quit attempts, and may even be less successful. Furthermore, girls who start smoking now will continue smoking four years longer, on average, than boys who start smoking. While information concerning gender differences in rates of smoking behaviors is useful, information concerning how gender may influence smoking initiation, maintenance, or cessation among adolescents is especially important to the development of more effective adolescent smoking interventions. To date, only a small number of studies have examined potential gender differences in how and why adolescents smoke or quit smoking.

Moreover, girls' greater interest in quitting smoking has not been sufficiently considered in the development of intervention programs.

One approach to broadening knowledge about potential gender differences in teen smoking is to focus exclusively on girls and explore factors that may be uniquely related to smoking behavior among adolescent females. This is the approach we take in the current paper. In the following pages, we examine the existing literature about smoking among teenage girls, with an emphasis on weight control motives, social influences, mood management motives, and image-related motives as particularly important factors in smoking among adolescent females.

FACTORS IN ADOLESCENT GIRLS' SMOKING

Weight Control

Among adolescents, smoking as a form of weight control appears to be a predominantly female phenomenon. This topic has been researched in several studies comparing boys' and girls' smoking, and findings have been consistent in documenting weight control motives as a particularly influential factor in adolescent females' smoking. Recent empirical and theoretical literature in the area is reviewed below.

Charlton (1984) compared boys' and girls' motives for smoking in a cross-sectional sample of 16,000 students from Northern England ranging in age from 9 to 19 years. Regardless of age or smoking status, girls were more likely than boys to agree that smoking controls weight. Among six-or-more-cigarettes-per-week smokers, 38.6% of boys and 46.0% of girls agreed that smoking keeps your weight down. Charlton concluded that weight "is of overwhelming importance to many people–especially young women" and noted that smoking indeed may be an effective method of keeping slim for some girls.

Camp, Klesges, and Relyea (1993) examined cross-sectionally how belief in smoking as a weight-control strategy may be related to adolescent smoking in a sample of 659 Catholic high school students. Although belief in smoking as a weight-control strategy did not distinguish never smokers from regular smokers, the weight-belief item did distinguish experimental smokers from regular smokers. Moreover, White girls were more likely to endorse the weight-belief item than White boys, Black boys, or Black girls. These researchers concluded that adolescent females, especially White females, are particularly susceptible to weight-control smoking, most likely because females are more vulnerable than males to pressures to be slim.

French, Perry, Leon, and Fulkerson (1994) examined cross-sectionally and prospectively the relations between weight concerns and dieting, and smoking behaviors in a sample of 1,705 7th-10th graders. For girls, four of six weight concerns and dieting symptoms were cross-sectionally associated with current smoking, and three of these six variables predicted smoking initiation over the course of one year. The presence of each of these symptoms and concerns approximately doubled the likelihood of current smoking or smoking initiation. For boys, only one weight concern (wish to be thin) was associated with current smoking, and none of the symptoms or concerns predicted smoking initiation. These researchers concluded that issues of weight concern are important determinants of girls' smoking and need to be addressed in smoking interventions targeted for adolescent females.

Waldron (1991) reviewed historical records from the turn of the century to the present to document and explain possible gender differences in smoking. She found that throughout the twentieth century a primary motivation for young women to smoke appears to be the desire to be slender. Waldron suggested recent increases in smoking among adolescent females have resulted from increases in attention to and emphasis on thinness for females. She concluded that weight control currently is an especially salient and socioculturally reinforced motive to smoke among adolescent girls.

Wolf (1991) made a similar argument using both feminist and developmental theory. She contended that sociocultural pressures for slimness exist for females of all ages, which lead some teenage girls to begin smoking as a weight management strategy. Moreover, she noted that adolescence is a developmental period during which concerns with appearance are particularly pronounced. Adolescent concern with appearance, combined with sociocultural pressures for feminine slimness and the potential effectiveness of smoking for weight control, may make teenage girls uniquely vulnerable to initiating smoking.

The notion that smoking can function as a weight control strategy appears to have some basis in reality. Research has demonstrated unequivocally that smokers weigh less than comparable non-smokers, and that smoking cessation is associated with weight gain (Grunberg, 1986). Such findings, as well as the apparent salience of smoking as a weight control strategy during the teenage years, highlight the need to address directly the relations between smoking and weight management in attempts to prevent or treat smoking among adolescents.

While it has been well established that smoking as a form of weight control appears to be especially common among adolescent girls, the existing literature on the topic is far from complete. van Roosmalen and McDaniel (1992) point out much work needs to be done examining how weight management motives for smoking may impact attempts to prevent or treat smoking among teenagers. Similarly, Waldron, Lye, and Brandon (1991) underscore the need to more fully understand how weight control expectancies for smoking are formed, under what conditions they can be contradicted, and under what conditions they lead to the initiation and maintenance of smoking among female adolescents. Moreover, French and Jeffery (1995) warn against unduly focusing on weight status or gender as risk factors for smoking, noting that the relations among weight control, smoking, and gender are complex and appear to be influenced by variables such as age and race/ethnicity.

Social Influences

Social influences have long been a focus of risk factor and intervention research in the adolescent substance use field, and a number of investigations have examined gender differences in the relations between peer and family influences and smoking. Several studies suggest the smoking attitudes and behaviors of peers and family may be more influential in girls' smoking than in boys' smoking. Recent empirical studies in the area are summarized below.

van Roosmalen and McDaniel (1992) compared boys' and girls' smoking attitudes and habits vis-à-vis the smoking attitudes and behaviors of their peers. In a sample of 1,689 eighth graders, these researchers found that teenage female smokers had a greater proportion of friends who smoke than did teenage male smokers. When their best friend smokes regularly, 77.8% of adolescent female smokers said they were not sure if they will quit smoking, versus 49.3% of adolescent male smokers. This finding extends to close friends of the opposite sex; female smokers with a close male friend who smokes were more likely to report that they were not sure if they will quit smoking than male smokers with a close female friend who smokes. Among adolescents who report that they have a best friend who smokes regularly, 62.4% of girls were smokers, and 56.6% of boys were smokers.

van Roosmalen and McDaniel also examined how familial smoking may affect the smoking attitudes and habits of adolescent boys and girls. Girls' smoking behavior was found to be more strongly associated with the smoking behaviors of their family members than was boys' smoking behavior. Moreover, pre-adolescent females were influenced more by same-gender role models than opposite-gender role models, while older girls appeared to be influenced by role models of both sexes.

Chassin, Presson, Sherman, Corty, and Olshavsky (1984) followed a sample of 2,818 sixth through eleventh graders for two years to examine the influences on social psychological variables on smoking transitions. In regard to social influences, participants who started smoking had greater numbers of parents and friends who smoked. These social influences were more important to the initiation of smoking than to the transition to regular smoking. Furthermore, girls' smoking transitions were better predicted by social influences than were boys' smoking transitions. In a further analysis of this same sample, Chassin, Presson, Sherman, Montello, and McGrew (1986) examined the importance of peer and parent variables in relation to smoking transitions over the course of one year. Initially nonsmoking adolescents with more smoking parents, more smoking peers, lower levels of parental support, and lower expectations of success from peers were more likely to begin smoking. Early stage smokers with more smoking friends, lower parental support, and higher levels of peer support were more likely to become regular smokers. When gender differences were examined, peer and parent influences proved significant for girls but not for boys.

Sarason, Mankowski, Peterson, and Dinh (1992) investigated adolescents' reasons for smoking in a sample of 1,615 tenth grade students. Two open-ended items assessed reasons for smoking: "Why did you smoke or try your first cigarette?" and "Why do you currently smoke?" Responses were coded into eleven *a priori* reasons for smoking, similar to those used in earlier research. In regard to current smoking, gender differences were found for one reason; girls were significantly more likely than boys to report smoking for pleasure and/or the reduction of negative affect. In regard to reasons for beginning to smoke, gender differences were found for two items: girls were significantly more likely than boys to report smoking because their friends did and because their friends pressured them to start. These findings are consistent with other studies suggesting girls' smoking is more strongly linked with peers' smoking than is boys' smoking.

Hu, Flay, Hedeker, Siddiqui, and Day (1995) examined longitudinally the relative importance of parental and friends' influences on adolescent smoking in large sample of middle school students followed from seventh grade through ninth grade. The associations between current smoking and friends' smoking, and between parental smoking and current smoking, were significant. When gender differences were examined, the influences of parental and friends' smoking were found to be greater for females than males. For both genders, the influence of friends' smoking was stronger than the influence of parental smoking. For females but not for males, the effects of friends' smoking on current smoking increased over time significantly. The authors concluded that girls may be more susceptible to social influences, and especially peer influences, than are boys.

Robinson, Klesges, Zbikowski, and Glaser (1997) investigated cross-sectionally the influence of a wide range of risk factors, including social influence variables, on different levels of cigarette use in a sample of 6,967 seventh graders. For females but not for males, smoking among family members distinguished nonsmokers from experimental smokers. For both genders, smoking among peers distinguished nonsmokers from experimental smokers. Regardless of gender, smoking among peers, but not smoking among family members, distinguished experimental smokers from regular smokers. These researchers concluded that smoking in the family has a greater influence on girls than on boys, and that smoking among peers has equal influence for both girls and boys.

Atkins, Wagner, and Gil (1999) examined gender differences in peer and family influences on adolescent smoking in a multi-ethnic sample of 867 middle school teenagers. Adolescents who had smoked, regardless of gender, reported having significantly more peers who smoked and who held positive smoking attitudes. Female smokers, but not male smokers, were more likely than nonsmokers to have parents who smoked and/or who held positive smoking attitudes. This finding was particularly pronounced for mothers, and distinguished female from male smokers. These researchers concluded that peer influences are important for the initiation of smoking for both boys and girls, and family influences are especially important for the initiation of smoking among girls.

Two additional recent studies did not find gender differences in peer influences on adolescent smoking. Urberg, Degirmencioglu, and Pilgrim (1997) examined the relative influences of closest friend's smoking and of friendship group's smoking on adolescents' cigarette smoking in a longitudinal study of 1,028 sixth, eighth and tenth graders. Closest friend's use was influential, albeit modestly, in the initiation of cigarette use. Friendship group's use, but not close friend's use, predicted the transition from smoking initiation to continued current cigarette use. Neither grade nor gender were related to the amount of influence, suggesting that peer influence on smoking during adolescence may operate similarly for different aged teenagers and for boys and girls. Stanton, Currie, Oei, and Silva (1996) followed a sample of 937 New Zealand 15-year-olds for three years to examine changes in social influence on smoking behavior. At 18 years of age, smoking was associated with having a close friend who smokes, having a significant other who smokes, and having a majority of smokers among one's friends. These associations did not vary as a function of gender, and were somewhat weaker than the relations found at age 15.

In sum, research concerning social influences on teenage smoking indicates that both boys' and girls' smoking is related to the smoking behavior and attitudes of their peers. Peer influence is strongest in the transition from experimental to regular smoking, and appears to increase through mid-adolescence, peaking between ages 15 to 18 years. There is some evidence that girls' smoking may be more strongly associated with peers' smoking behavior and attitudes than is boys' smoking, but three recent studies found no gender differences in the association between peer influences and smoking. Additional studies are needed to clarify whether gender differences exist in peer influences on smoking among teenagers.

Research concerning familial influences on teenage smoking suggests that girls' smoking is more strongly associated with family members' smoking behavior and attitudes than is boys' smoking, and this relation appears to be particularly strong among younger girls in relation to same-sex family members. Moreover, parental influence appears to be greatest for the transition from nonsmoking to smoking initiation.

In an attempt to explain gender differences in parental influence, van Roosmalen and McDaniel (1992) have argued that adolescent females have closer bonds and intimacy ties to family than do adolescent males, and thus are more influenced by their parents. However, much more work needs to be done to test this model and examine how it may impact attempts to prevent or treat smoking among female and male teenagers. Moreover, more research is needed concerning the mechanisms by which peers and family influences may differentially affect boys' and girls' smoking (e.g., modeling, shaping smoking expectancies, peer conformity, etc.), and strategies through which the association between social influences and boys' and girls' smoking may be contravened.

Management of Negative Mood

Among adults, major depression, whether historical, current, or subsyndromal, is strongly associated with cigarette smoking (Borrelli, Bock, King, & Pinto, 1996; Glassman, 1993). Adult smokers have higher rates of major depressive disorder and demonstrate more depressive symptoms than nonsmokers (Anda et al., 1990; Breslau, Kilbey, & Andreski., 1991; Glassman et al., 1990; Kendler et al., 1993). Moreover, adult smokers with depressive symptoms have greater difficulty in attempts to quit smoking, demonstrate more severe withdrawal profiles, and are more likely to relapse to smoking following cessation treatment (Covey, Glassman, & Sterner, 1990; Madden et al., 1997). However, recent studies suggest that the relation between smoking and depression may exist primarily for only the most nicotine addicted smokers (Madden et al., 1997)

Borrelli et al. (1996) have enumerated how major depression may influence smoking behavior and attempts at cessation among females. First, beginning in adolescence, depression is twice as common in women as in men. Second, as described in the preceding paragraph, depression and negative affect have been associated with smoking, nicotine addiction, and smoking cessation failure. Third, quitting smoking is especially difficult during the phases of the reproductive cycle associated with greater levels of dysphoria. Fourth, subgroups of women who have a high risk of sustained smoking also have a high risk of developing depression. While all, some, or none of these factors may explain smoking among certain subgroups of women, it has been clearly established that negative affect and smoking are strongly related in adulthood.

In studies of adolescents, similar relations between negative affect and smoking have been found. Both cross-sectional and longitudinal studies have shown that smoking is significantly more prevalent among adolescents with a history of depression or depressive symptoms than among adolescents without such characteristics (Covey & Tam, 1990; Hawkins, Hawkins, & Seeley, 1992; Brown, Lewinsohn, Seeley, & Wagner, 1996). Given these findings and the well-documented gender differences in the prevalence of depression, two recent investigations have examined how gender may influence relations between negative affect and smoking during adolescence.

Choi, Patten, Gillin, Kaplan, and Pierce (1997) examined longitudinally the degree to which adolescent cigarette smoking is associated with the development of depressive symptoms. A large sample of adolescents (n = 6,863), without depressive symptoms at baseline, were followed for twelve months. As expected, there were marked gender differences in the development of depressive symptoms, with 15.3% of girls and 8.1% of boys manifesting clinical symptoms. However, there were no gender differences in the degree of association between depression and smoking. For both genders, smoking status was the most significant predictor of developing notable depressive symptoms.

Patton, Hibbert, Rosier, Carlin, Caust, and Bowes (1996) examined cross-sectionally the associations between depression and anxiety symptoms and teenage smoking transitions in a sample of 956 seventh, 911 ninth, and 658 eleventh graders in Australia. The relations between depression and anxiety symptoms and regular smoking was modest, though evident, for teenage males, but substantial for teenage females. Girls with high levels of symptoms demonstrated an almost four-fold increase in regular smoking compared with girls with low levels of symptoms. In contrast, boys with high levels of symptoms were 1.7 times as likely to be regular smokers than boys with low levels of symptoms. Moreover, girls were twice as likely as boys to fall into a high symptom group, regardless of smoking status.

In sum, depression and smoking have been shown to be related in adolescents, with smoking adolescents more likely to develop depressive symptoms, and depressed and anxious adolescents more likely to be current smokers. While adolescent females are more likely to be or become depressed than are adolescent males, both female and male teenagers with depressive affect are at elevated risk for smoking. It remains unclear whether the strength of association between negative affect and smoking in adolescence varies by gender. What is clear is that adolescent girls, because they are more likely than adolescent boys to experience depressive symptoms, are especially vulnerable to begin smoking in response to depressive and negative affect.

These findings, along with the findings from the adult literature, are consistent with a self-medication model for smoking. In brief, the model holds that nicotine use represents an attempt to cope with psychological distress and negative affect (Patton, Hibbert, Rosier et al., 1996). The subjective effects of smoking (i.e., the self-medication effects) can include anxiety reduction, concentration improvement, mood elevation, and the facilitation of social communication (Glass, 1990; West, 1993). Another mechanism by which depression may increase the risk of smoking is through its association with lowered self-esteem and self-confidence, which may make depressed youth particularly vulnerable to social influences to smoke (Patton et al., 1996). These potential mechanisms have not been well researched with adolescents, and deserve further attention.

Regardless of the mechanism of association between negative affect and smoking, the adult literature clearly indicates that the presence of depressive symptoms decreases smokers' success in quitting smoking (Borrelli et al., 1996). However, it remains unknown how depression may affect adolescent smokers' responses to intervention; research is needed which examines how depression and negative affect may influence interest in quitting, willingness to enter into smoking cessation intervention, adherence to smoking cessation programs, and outcome and relapse rates following intervention. An important additional focus should be how gender may influence teenage smokers' responses to intervention.

Image-Related Motivations

Vulnerability on the part of females to image-related smoking motivations has been suggested as another factor that may contribute to gender differences in smoking (Royce, Corbett, Sorensen, & Ockene, 1997; Waldron, 1991). According to this model, women tend to be more sensitive to and influenced by stereotypes related to smoking than are men. Stated another way, females may be more likely than males to adopt and maintain smoking if smoker stereotypes are perceived as consistent with or as more desirable than one's self-image.

Targeted advertising for cigarettes has attempted to exploit this possibility. Research has demonstrated that cigarette advertisements are specifically designed for certain target markets, with horseplay and sexual appeal advertisements used more often with female audiences (Basil, Schooler, Altman, & Slater, 1991). These smoker characteristics may be seen as especially desirable among certain groups of women, who thus may be more inclined to smoke. To date, possible gender differences in vulnerability to image-related smoking motivations have received more attention in the theoretical literature than in the empirical literature. However, two recent studies from the same group of investigators have examined whether adolescent boys and girls differ in image-related smoking motivations.

Aloise-Young and Hennigan (1996) investigated cross-sectionally the role of self-consistency and self-enhancement motives for smoking in a sample of 1,971 fifth through eighth graders. Self-consistency motives involve individuals smoking because their self-image is similar to their image of a smoker. In contrast, self-enhancement motives involve individuals smoking to improve their image (i.e., to move their self-image closer to their image of a smoker). For both seventh and eighth grade female participants, self-image and smoker stereotypes were significantly closer to one another than for younger and male participants, specifically in regard to the traits of "coolness" and sociability. For females but not males, the self-enhancement model also was supported. Girls who rated themselves more negatively than smoker stereotypes had significantly higher levels of lifetime smoking than girls who rated themselves at least as positively as smoker stereotypes, specifically in regard to the trait of coolness. According to the authors, these findings suggest that adolescent females may be more vulnerable to image-related smoking motivations than males. In a one-year follow-up of this same sample, Aloise-Young, Hennigan, and Graham (1996) found support for self-consistency motivations predicting longitudinally the onset of smoking. However, no gender differences were found in any of the longitudinal analyses.

In sum, it appears that image-related smoking motivations play a role in adolescents' smoking, and this role may be stronger among girls than among boys. However, considerable work remains to be done to document the degree to which gender influences vulnerability to image-related smoking motivations, and how such motivations may interact with other factors that increase the risk of adolescents initiating and maintaining smoking (e.g., peer influences, negative affect). Moreover, the question of how image-related smoking motivations may interact with attempts to prevent or treat smoking among adolescents has yet to be explored.

PREVENTION AND INTERVENTION FOR GIRLS

Brief Summary of Current Approaches

Several approaches to preventing and treating smoking among adolescents are currently in use. None of these approaches are specific to females, though many may be effective for addressing smoking among girls. Below, we summarize some of the more popular teen smoking prevention and intervention programs, though we must acknowledge in advance the notable absence of summaries of smoking cessation programs for teens. To date, the treatment of nicotine addiction among adolescents has been a neglected topic in the empirical literature (for an exception, see Myers, Brown, & Kelly, this publication). We conclude this section with suggestions concerning how programs might be customized for use with girls.

Drug Abuse Resistance Education (D.A.R.E.) is one of the most common alcohol, tobacco, and other drugs prevention programs (Ennett, Rosenbaum, Flewelling, Bieler, Ringwalt, & Bailey, 1994). D.A.R.E. involves a collaboration between local police departments and school systems, and is a seventeen-week program helping children from kindergarten to sixth grade recognize and resist pressures to use alcohol, tobacco, and other drugs (Bureau of Justice Assistance, 1988). Participation in the D.A.R.E. program includes: completion of the workbook exercises; having good attendance; demonstrating appropriate behavior in class; writing an essay; keeping drug free; and helping out with a drug-prevention project at school. While police departments and school systems have been enthusiastic proponents of D.A.R.E., recent evaluations of its effectiveness have suggested students who participate in the program are no less likely to use or abuse alcohol, tobacco, or other drugs than students who do not participate (Clayton, Leukefeld, Harrington, & Cattarello, 1996; Dukes, Stein, & Ullman, 1997; Ennett et al., 1994; Hansen & McNeal, 1997; Zagumny & Thompson, 1997). Nonetheless, the D.A.R.E. program is in wide use across the country, and represents an approach to prevention that may benefit some students in its current form. Currently, there is no reason to believe that the program may be more or less effective for boys versus girls. D.A.R.E. has the potential to impact the smoking behavior of a large number of students, but recent evaluations suggest considerable revision is needed before D.A.R.E. can make a significant impact on adolescents' smoking behavior.

A prevention program with demonstrated effectiveness for reducing tobacco use among adolescents is Life Skills Training (LST) (Botvin, 1996; Botvin, Dusenbury, Baker, & James-Ortiz, 1992; Botvin & Epstein, 1999). LST is a multi-session, cognitive-behavioral prevention approach geared to junior high and middle school students. It is designed to (a) affect drug-related expectancies, (b) teach skills for resisting social influences to use drugs, and (c) promote the development of general personal self-management and social skills. Unlike more traditional prevention approaches (e.g., D.A.R.E.), the emphasis is on the development of skills associated with decreased risk for using substances, and little time is spent on the long-term consequences of alcohol, tobacco, and other drug use. Other skills-based intervention programs, especially those designed to teach adolescent-relevant skills for managing social influences for substance use (e.g., Project Towards No Tobacco Use), have been shown to be similarly effective for decreasing smoking among adolescents (Sussman, Dent, Stacy, Sun, Craig, Simon, Burton, & Flay, 1993). It also is noteworthy that gender has not been found to be a significant predictor of response to skills-based interventions, indicating that these programs are equally effective for boys and girls.

Preventive measures via the juvenile justice system represent another intervention not specific to teenage girls but in wide use across the country. It is illegal across all fifty states for a person under the age of eighteen to use or purchase tobacco products. In Florida, it is a misdemeanor for a minor to smoke a cigarette. If a minor is caught using tobacco products, the local authorities will issue them a Notice To Appear (NTA), which mandates a court appearance accompanied by parent(s) or guardian(s). For a first time smoking violation, the offender must complete sixteen hours of community service or pay a fine, and must attend a school-approved anti-tobacco program. If the court date is missed, an arrest warrant is issued. A second violation within twelve weeks of the first violation is punishable by a twenty-five dollar fine. A third violation within the first twelve weeks can lead to withholding or suspending the minor's driving privilege. The effectiveness of these legal measures has not been well studied, but supporters point to a recent reduction in cigarette use among Florida adolescents as partial evidence of their success.

Recommendations

As noted above, the most commonly employed approaches to preventing and treating adolescent smoking are not gender-specific, and appear to be equally effective (or ineffective) for boys and girls. Epidemiological data indicate that female smokers are more likely than male smokers to attempt to quit smoking during high school, and this suggests that teenage girls may be especially receptive to interventions in support of their cessation attempts.

Some researchers have suggested that smoking prevention and cessation programs may demonstrate increased effectiveness with adolescent females if a component devoted to healthier and more effective methods of weight control is included. As described earlier, adolescents who report smoking to control weight are primarily female, and this motive appears to be one of the most important reasons that girls report for smoking. To date, there have been no published reports concerning the development or testing of such a component. We believe that a customizable component emphasizing healthy nutrition, healthy dieting habits, and effective non-smoking alternatives to weight control may prove helpful in preventing or treating smoking among girls. This topic is ripe for investigation.

It also has been suggested that prevention and treatment programs for adolescent girls need to pay greater attention to potential social influences on smoking. As described earlier, smoking behaviors and attitudes among peers and especially family members may be more strongly associated with smoking among teenage girls than with smoking among teenage boys. While many smoking prevention and treatment programs for adolescents have included attention to social influences, most of this attention has been in the form of teaching gender-universal refusal skills to adolescents. Little has been done focusing on social influence factors that may be especially important in girls' smoking, such as susceptibility to social influences or working with friendship networks that reinforce and maintain smoking behavior. More basic and applied research is needed in this area. Moreover, there rarely has been any involvement of family members in prevention or treatment programs for teenage smoking. Given the relative importance of parent and sibling influences in adolescent girls' lives, we believe that an important area for future research and development is how to affect and involve family members in efforts to prevent and treat smoking among adolescent girls.

A third area that has been identified as holding potential for improving smoking interventions for adolescent girls is attention to depression and negative affect. As reviewed earlier, adolescent females are twice as likely as adolescent males to experience depression, depressed teenagers are more likely to smoke than nondepressed teenagers, and adolescent smokers are more likely to be depressed than adolescent nonsmokers. While depression and smoking are related for both genders, the fact that more girls are or will become depressed makes this relation especially important in smoking among female adolescents. We believe that an important area for future research and development is the incorporation of a negative mood management component in programs devoted to preventing and treating smoking among adolescent girls.

A final area that should be considered in attempts to improve smoking interventions for girls is the role of image-related smoking motivations in smoking initiation and maintenance. Adolescents who hold smoker stereotypes that are consistent with or more desirable than their self-images are more likely to smoke, and girls may be more vulnerable to image-related smoking motivations than are boys. As noted by Aloise-Young and Hennigan (1996), an important direction for future prevention and treatment efforts is to attempt to manipulate adolescents' stereotypes about smokers to make them less consistent with and less desirable than adolescents' self-images. In regard to girls, this may mean directly targeting smoker stereotypes along the dimensions of "coolness" and sociability, as well teaching them skills to recognize and resist targeted cigarette advertisements that use "horseplay" and sex appeal to sell cigarettes to females.

REFERENCES

Aloise-Young, P., & Hennigan, K. (1996). Self-image, the smoker stereotype and cigarette smoking: Developmental patterns from fifth through eighth grade. *Journal of Adolescence, 19*, 163-177.

Aloise-Young, P., Hennigan, K., & Graham, J. (1996). Role of the self-image and smoker stereotype in smoking onset during early adolescence: A longitudinal study. *Health Psychology, 15*, 494-497.

Anda, R.F., Williamson, D.F., Escobedo, L.G., Mast, E.E., Giovino, G.A, & Remington, P.L. (1990). Depression and the dynamics of smoking: A national perspective. *JAMA, 264*, 1541-1545.

Atkins, J.H., Wagner, E. & Gil, A. (1999, November). Gender differences in social influences on adolescent smoking. Paper to be presented at the 33rd Annual Converntion of the Association for Advancement of Behavior Therapy, Toronto, ONT, CAN.

Basil, M.D., Schooler, C., Altman, D.G. & Slater, M. (1991). How cigarettes are advertised in magazines: Special messages for special markets. *Health Communication, 3*, 75-91.

Borrelli, B., Bock, B., King, T., & Pinto, B. (1996). The impact of depression on smoking cessation in women. *American Journal of Preventive Medicine, 12*, 378-387.

Botvin, G.J. (1996). Substance abuse prevention through life skills training. In R. DeV. Peters, R.J. McMahon (Eds.). *Preventing childhood disorders, substance abuse, and delinquency.* Banff international behavioral science series, Vol. 3. (pp. 215-240). Thousand Oaks, CA: Sage.

Botvin, G.J., & Epstein, J.A. (1999). Preventing cigarette smoking among children and adolescents. D.F. Seidman & L.S. Covey (Eds) *Helping the hard-core smoker: A clinician's guide* (pp. 51-71). Mahwah, NJ: Lawrence Erlbaum Associates.

Botvin, G.J., Dusenbury, L., Baker, E., & James-Ortiz, S. (1992). Smoking prevention among urban minority youth: Assessing effects on outcome and mediating variables. *Health Psychology, 11*, 290-299.

Breslau, N., Kilbey, M., & Andreski, P. (1991). Nicotine dependence, and anxiety in young adults. *Archives of General Psychiatry, 48*, 1069-1074.

Brown. R.A., Lewinsohn, P.M., Seeley, J.R., & Wagner, E.F. (1996). Cigarette smoking, major depression, and other psychiatric disorders among adolescents. *Journal of the American Academy of Child and Adolescent Psychiatry, 35*, 1602-1610.

Bureau of Justice Assistance, U.S. Department of Justice. (1988). *Implementing Project DARE: Drug Abuse Resistance Education.* Washington, DC: Bureau of Justice Assitance.

Camp, D., Klesges, R., & Relyea, G. (1993). The relationship between body weight concerns and adolescent smoking. *Heath psychology, 12*, 24-32.

Centers for Disease Control (1998). Selected cigarette smoking initiation and quitting behaviors among high school students–United States, 1997. *Morbidity and Mortality Weekly Report, 47*, 386-389.

Charlton, A. (1984). Smoking and weight control in teenagers. *Public Health London, 98*, 277-281.

Chassin, L., Presson, C., Rose, J., & Sherman, S. (1996). The natural history of cigarette smoking from adolescence to adulthood: Demographic predictors of continuity and change. *Health Psychology, 15*, 478-484.

Chassin, L., Presson, C., Sherman, S., Corty, E., & Olvashavsky, R. (1984). Predicting the onset of cigarette smoking in adolescents: A longitudinal study. *Journal of Applied Social Psychology, 14*, 224-243.

Chassin, L., Presson, C., Sherman, S., Montello, D., & McGrew, J. (1986). Changes in peer and parent influence during adolescence: Longitudinal versus cross-sectional perspectives on smoking initiation. *Developmental Psychology, 22,* 327-334.

Choi, W.S., Patten, C.A., Gillin, J.C., Kaplan, R.M., & Pierce, J.P. (1997). Cigarette smoking predicts development of depressive symptoms among U.S. adolescents. *Annals of Behavioral Medicine, 19,* 42-50.

Clayton, R.R., Leukefeld, C.G., Harrington, N.G., & Cattarello, A. (1996). D.A.R.E. (Drug Abuse Resistance Education): Very popular but not very effective. In C.B. McCoy& L.R. Metsch (Eds.) *Intervening with drug-involved youth* (pp. 101-109) Thousand Oaks, CA: Sage Publications, Inc.

Covey, L.S., Glassman, A.H., & Sterner, F. (1990). Depression and depressive symptoms in smoking cessation. *Comprehensive Psychiatry, 31,* 350-354.

Covey, L.S., & Tam, D. (1990). Depressive mood, the single-parent home, and adolescent cigarette smoking. *American Journal of Public Health, 80,* 1330-1333.

Dukes, R.L., Stein, J.A., & Ullman, J.B. (1997). Long-term impact of Drug Abuse Resistance Education (D. A. R. E.): Results of a 6-year follow-up. *Evaluation Review, 21,* 483-500.

Ennett, S.T., Rosenbaum, D.P., Flewelling, R.L., Bieler, G.S., Ringwalt, C.L., & Bailey, S.L. (1994). Long-term evaluation of drug abuse resistance education. *Addictive Behaviors, 19,* 113-125.

French, S., & Jeffery, R. (1995). Weight concerns and smoking: A literature review. *Annals of Behavioral Medicine, 17,* 234-244.

French, S.A., Perry, C.L., Leon, G.R., & Fulkerson, J.A. (1994). Weight concerns, dieting behavior, and smoking initiation among adolescents: A prospective study. *American Journal of Public Health, 84,* 1818-1820.

Glass, R.M. (1990). Blue mood, blackened lungs, depression and smoking. *Journal of the American Medical Association, 264,* 1583-1584.

Glassman, A.H. (1993). Cigarette smoking: Implications for psychiatric illness. *American Journal of Psychiatry, 150,* 546-553.

Glassman, A.H., Helzer, J.E., Covey, L.S., Cottler, L.B., Stetner, F., Tipp, J.E., & Johnson, J. (1990). Smoking, smoking cessation, and major depression. *Journal of the American Medical Association, 264,* 1546-1549.

Grunberg, N.E. (1986). Behavioral and biological factors in the relationship between tobacco use and body weight. In E.S. Katkin & S.B. Manuck (Eds.), *Advances in Behavioral Medicine* (Vol. 2, pp. 97-129). Greenwich, CT: JAI Press.

Hansen, W.B., & McNeal, R.B. (1997). How D.A.R.E. works: An examination of program effects on mediating variables. *Health Education & Behavior, 24,* 165-176.

Hawkins, W.E., Hawkins, M.J., & Seeley, J.R. (1992). Stress, health-related behavior and quality of life on depressive symptomatology in a sample of adolescents. *Psychological Reports, 71,* 183-186.

Hu, F., Flay, B., Hedeker, D. & Day, L. (1995). The influences of friends' and parental smoking on adolescent smoking behavior: The effects of time and prior smoking. *Journal of Applied Social Psychology, 25,* 2018-2947.

Johnston, L.D., O'Malley, P.M., & Bachman, J.G. (1998). *National survey results on drug use from the Monitoring the Future Study, 1975-1997* Volume 1 Secondary School Students. (National Institute on Drug Abuse NIH Publication No. 98-4345). Washington, DC: U.S. Government Printing Office.

Kendler, K.S., Neale, M.C., MacLean, C.J., Heath, A.C., Eaves, L.J., & Kessler, R.C. (1993). Smoking and major depression: A causal analysis. *Archives of General Psychiatry, 50,* 36-43.

Khoury, E., Warheit, G., Zimmerman, R., Vega, W., & Gil, A. (1996). Gender and ethnic differences in the prevalence of alcohol, cigarette, and illicit drug use over time in a cohort of young Hispanic adolescents in South Florida. *Women & Health, 24,* 21-40.

Krupka, L.R., & Vener, A.M. (1992). Gender differences in drug (prescription, non-prescription, alcohol and tobacco) advertising: Trends and implications. *Journal of Drug Issues, 22,* 339-360.

Madden, P.A.F., Bucholz, K.K., Dinwiddie, S.H., Slutske, W.S., Bierut, L.J., Statham, D.J., Dunne, M.P., Martin, N.C., Heath, A.C. (1997). Nicotine withdrawal in women. *Addiction, 92,* 889-902.

Patton, G.C., Hibbert, M., Rosier, M.J., Carlin, J.B., Caust, J., & Bowes, G. (1996). Is smoking associated with depression and anxiety in teenagers? *American Journal of Public Health, 86,* 225-230.

Pierce, J., & Gilpin, F. (1996). How long will today's new adolescent smoker be addicted to cigarettes? *American Journal of Public Health, 86,* 253-256.

Robinson, L.A., Klesges, R.C., Zbikowski, S.M., & Glaser, R. (1997). Predictors of risk for different stages of adolescent smoking in a biracial sample. *Journal of Consulting and Clinical Psychology, 65,* 653-662.

Royce, J., Corbett, K., Sorensen, G., & Ockene, J. (1997). Gender, social pressure, and smoking cessations: The community intervention trial for smoking cessation (commit) at baseline. *Social Science Medicine, 3,* 359-270.

Sarason, I., Mankowski, E., Peterson, A., & Dinh, K. (1992). Adolescents' reasons for smoking. *Journal of School Health, 62,* 185-190.

Stanton, W., Currie, G., Oei, T., & Silva, P. (1996). A developmental approach to influences on adolescents' smoking and quitting. *Journal of Applied Developmental Psychology, 17,* 307-319.

Stanton, W., Lowe, J., & Gillespie, A. (1996). Adolescents' experiences of smoking cessation. *Drug and Alcohol Dependence, 43,* 63-70.

Sussman, S., Dent, C., Severson, H., Burton, D., & Flay, B. (1998). Self-initiated quitting among adolescent smokers. *Preventive Medicine, 27,* A19-A28.

Sussman, S., Dent, C.W., Stacy, A.W., Sun, P., Craig, S., Simon, T.R., Burton, D., & Flay, B.R. (1993). Project towards no tobacco use: 1-year behavior outcomes. *American Journal of Public Health, 83,* 1245-1250.

University of Michigan. (1998). *Smoking among American teens declines some.* News and Information Services Press Release, December 18, 1998.

Urberg, K.A., Degirmencioglu, S.R., & Pilgrim. C. (1997). Close friend and group influence on adolescent cigarette smoking and alcohol use. *Developmental Psychology, 33,* 834-844.

van Roosmalen, E. & McDaniel, S. (1989). Peer group influence as a factor in smoking behavior of adolescents. *Adolescence, 96,* 801-816.

van Roosmalen, E. & McDaniel, S. (1992). Adolescent smoking intentions: Gender differences in peer context. *Adolescence, 27,* 87-105.

Waldron, I. (1991). Patterns and causes of gender differences in smoking. *Social Science Medicine, 32,* 989-1005.

Waldron, I., Lye, D., & Brandon, A. (1991). Gender differences in teenage smoking. *Women and Health, 17*, 65-90.

Wolf, N. (1991). *The beauty myth.* Toronto, ON: Random House of Canada Limited.

West, R. (1993). Beneficial effects of nicotine: Fact or fiction? *Addiction, 88*, 589-590.

Zagumny, M.J., & Thompson, M.K. (1997). Does D.A.R.E. work? An evaluation in rural Tennessee. *Journal of Alcohol & Drug Education, 42*, 32-41.

Index

Adolescent females, smoking by, 93-100
  cotinine levels in, 36-37
  factors influencing
    depression, 56,101-102
    image, 102-103,106
    management of negative mood, 100-102
    social influences, 97-100
    weight control, 95-97,106
  prevalence, 93-94
  smoking prevention and treatment for, 39,94,103-106
  subjective effects experienced by, 35
  withdrawal symptoms in, 34
Adult smokers
  nicotine-dependent, 37
  smoking cessation strategies of, 15, 16
Advertising
  of cigarettes, targeted for females, 102
  of nicotine replacement therapy, 19
  of smokeless tobacco, 14
African-American adolescents
  smoking prevalence trends among, 8
  smoking progression in, 40
African Americans, projected smoking-related deaths among, 8
Agency for Health Care Policy and Research, nicotine replacement therapy guidelines of, 54
Age of onset
  of drug abuse, 12
  of nicotine dependence, 55
  of smoking initiation, 2,28

implication for smoking cessation, 12-13
Aggressive behavior, of adolescent smokers, 56
Alcohol abuse treatment, of smokers, 78
Alcohol use, by smokers, 78
  by cigar smokers, 8
American Medical Association, 67,68
Anger, as withdrawal symptom, 34
Antidepressants, as smoking cessation aid, 18,20
Anxiety
  as nicotine withdrawal symptom, 29
  as smoking risk factor, gender differences in, 101
Anxiety, of adolescent smokers, 56
Aschenbach Child Behavior Checklist, 56
Attitudes, toward smoking, as smoking risk factor, 99

Behavioral interventions, for smoking cessation, combined with nicotine replacement therapy, 54-55,67-68,69
Boredom alleviation, as smoking motivation, 15,39
Brain, effect of nicotine on, 58-59
Bronchitis, smoking-related, 52
Brown, Sandra, 82
Bupropion, as smoking cessation aid, 18,20

Carbon monoxide
  as cigarette smoke component, 59-60

8242